The Church Does Not Exist

(but something better does!)

Tom Mann

Scripture quotations taken from the New American Standard Bible®,
Copyright © 1960, 1962, 1963, 1968, 1971, 1972, 1973,
1975, 1977, 1995 by The Lockman Foundation
Used by permission. (www.Lockman.org)

ISBN: 0615865585
ISBN-13: 978-0615865584

DEDICATION

Beautiful souls are found in places sometimes where you least expect to find them. They may appear like delicate flowers in Alpine islands surrounded by fields of snow. This book is dedicated to my wife Meladie, my sister Robin and her daughter Courtney and my brother's daughter, Marcy. Because they were seeking for more and trying to grow toward the light, they were the reason for my writing this book. It is possible to grow in what the world views as the most unlikely places and in the most unlikely ways, when in reality such rich growth is only possible in such environments. Plants searching for water in dry places put down the deepest roots. These women are the precious blooms appearing in unexpected places. Beautiful daughters of Abraham, this is for you.

CONTENTS

ACKNOWLEDGMENTS

Much of what I have learned has come from unlearning. Two men have helped me unlearn and then learn again. Ed Culp helped me to have a fresh view of things. His earnest searching has caused me and others to look at things with fresh eyes. He has started me toward understanding things more clearly. Dan Moody demonstrated God's love in action. He is a confidante who listens without judging. Dan has taught me how to listen and love without judgment. He's helped me to view myself afresh. He gave me hope. These two men have helped me see the world and see myself in God's terms. Because of them, my anticipation of the awe of the next horizon takes away my breath. They are heroes of faith whom I can never repay.

This book I owe to my "called" sister, Robin. John said, "See how great a love the Father has bestowed on us, that we would be called children of God; and such we are." Through the providence of God she was adopted into God's family and especially into my family. She was "called" to be my sister and is truly "called" my sister. My beautiful little sister has kept me on my toes and is really the reason I wrote this book. Her questions for me have made me question and think harder than I would have on my own. She was searching harder than I was at times and more earnestly than most Christians I know. Her search continues. God has blessed me with a physical and spiritual sibling with whom I can trade thoughts and ideas without judgment.

A special thanks goes to my brother in the faith, George Wark. He has been a blessing I cannot comprehend fully. Without his fine-toothed comb proofreading of this book, I would never have felt comfortable moving ahead. His dispassionate review has saved me from many embarrassing lapses in grammar and judgment. George has also pointed me into deeper understandings of things that I already "knew," even though I did not. He is a true fellow worker in Christ. I pray that God will prosper him.

My amazing wife has understood things I have not. Meladie has been my sounding board, my confidante, and my constant encouragement. Her constant questioning has been my primary source of inspiration. She helped me reconsider everything. She has been my editor and proofreader. In a large way, this book is as much hers as it is mine. She, and she alone has critiqued by constant verbal ramblings and gave order to my thoughts. What a blessing, what a help, she has been to me and to the cause of God's kingdom. While I threw words on pages, she was the force that gave them sense and order.

One last point is that I occasionally refer only to a chapter and not to "chapter and verse." This is intentional. First chapters and verses can be very arbitrary dissections. Secondly, I am laying down a personal challenge for you to look at the Scriptures for yourself and not rely on me citing proof text after proof text. Ultimately, you are responsible for what you believe and what you practice. God has blessed me with gifts; however, infallibility is not one of them. Test. Try. Examine. Prove.

Thanks to you all. Praise to Yahveh[1] for putting you all in my life. I pray that this will all be to His glory. All praise belongs to Yahveh, the source of all that has been, is, and will be. How incomprehensibly magnificent is He.

Tom Mann

---

[1] The tetragrammaton for God's name is יהוה, which is commonly transliterated as YHWH; however, probably the more accurate transliteration is YHVH, which is used throughout this work.

PREFACE

First, *The Church Does Not Exist* is written for Christians. If you are an unbeliever, this book may appear to be riddled with quibbles about words, contradictions and hypocrisy. If you are not a Christian, I would not expect you to comprehend some of the points. Even extremely orthodox Christians may believe this book to be nonsense at times. This book was not written for either extreme.

Second, if you are a Christian, and you see no problem with where you are and what you are doing, this book is also not for you. The purpose of this book is to bring richness to Christians' lives who are uncomfortable and searching. Perhaps by reading this little book, you may begin to have a new view of institutional religion. If you are already discontent, you have the choice of continuing to be discouraged or being teased along in your quest to know God better. I hope to tease you.

I am going out on a limb in this work. People I love dearly will be certain that I am sawing away the very tree limb I am sitting on and will fall to my peril. Others may see this work as my pruning dead branches to help the tree thrive. Others may still see me as girding the trunk of the Church with the aim of killing it: I am not. If God's kingdom grows as a result of this work, it will be obvious which branches were being pruned.

This book has a chatty style. Purposefully. Many people are put off by stylistic and grammatical snobbery: I have purposefully tried to desnob my writing. I may be lambasted for my lack of scholastic support: that's okay. I am not pulling things out of thin air. If I grasp for other men and women to validate my thoughts they only contribute – ultimately – to the pride of life. "I must be right if someone else agrees with me" is a philosophical trap of human pride and weakness. This work has few footnotes: I purposefully omitted many. I am violating the style of my academic and legal background. I did this to challenge you to look for yourself. Challenge my thoughts. Think for yourself! Don't try to shoot down "my truth" (as though I have any of my own); seek The Truth. Don't look for *my* God or *your* God, look for *the* God.

We need to make a distinction between the Church and the *ekklesia*. Throughout this little book, Church will refer to that "thing" that humans have mutated from God's original masterpiece. Many Christians have tried to disclaim their connection to institutionalized religion by using a lower case "c" in Church: this is a distinction without a difference. At the beginning of this book, I use the word *ekklesia* as we search for a better word to describe God's original design.

Admiral Chester W. Nimitz said, "God grant me the courage not to give up what I think is right even though I think it is hopeless." On a personal note, the very idea of changing another person's attitude, much less a large number of people's attitudes, seems hopeless. If I were the only person doing this, I would agree. However, throughout all Christianity, there is a longing for a richer connection with God and with fellow saints. There is a broad dissatisfaction with the status quo. I am convinced that the rich, deep connection with God and with our fellow Christians cannot grow properly in the institution of the Church. Many Christians are root-bound by trying to grow in a small container, a Church. Some people may be satisfied with being a bonsai. Although I believe what I am writing to be right, my real quest is for the truth: therein lies my hope. Albert Einstein said, "Learn from yesterday, live for today, hope for tomorrow. The important thing is not to stop questioning." As a Christian, the important thing is to continually seek God and His glory. God is a rewarder of those who seek Him – a continual process throughout our lives until He blesses us to be in His presence. Hebrews 11. Then we will know even as were are known. Only then will seeking end.

Tom Mann
611 Herchel Drive
Temple Terrace, Florida 33617
packmann@me.com

PART ONE: THE PROBLEM

1: TRAILS OF OUR FATHERS

Arizona's Grand Canyon National Park is a beautiful place. It is an amazing geologic display of God's grandeur and power. Hundreds of thousands of people visit the park every year. Most visitors see the canyon only from the south rim: they look across the seven miles to the opposite rim and the one mile down to the bottom. A few get to view the canyon from the bottom up, by hiking, rafting or riding mules. What looks like a small outcropping of rocks from the top turns out to be a colorful, towering spire of boulders from below. How do visitors get down to the bottom? It would be folly if someone thought he could pick his own route down a cliff face safely. Visitors may only go down to the bottom on only the few trails that have been established by the Park Rangers.

Searching. I have been blessed to have hiked through the canyon twice, once with my son and his friends when he was a teenager. My favorite trail is not really a trail at all. It is called the Escalante Route. It is called a route rather than a trail because the way varies according to the season and height of the river and goes ways that most people would not think of as a trail. Rather than following painted signs as many hiking trails do, this route is marked by cairns, pyramid-shaped stacks of rocks. Park rangers regularly hike the route and set out the safe way to go by piling small rocks on top of larger ones. In some places the cairns lead from boulder to boulder along the Colorado River. In other places they lead up cliff faces or down rock slides.

Often it is difficult to see where the "trail" is. Finding a particular pile of rocks in a canyon full of rocks can be intimidating. When weather, animals or other careless hikers knock the cairns over, just finding the path can be a huge challenge. I have spent a long time scouring the landscape for a cairn so I could determine which fragile outcropping will lead off a gravel ridge to safety, rather than all the others that lead out into oblivion. When hiking across a broad mesa, the dangers are fewer. But, the route often followed paths no wider than two feet along a cliff face with a drop of hundreds of feet to the river below. The first time I hiked the Escalante Route, I prayed a lot. When I was with my teenaged son and his friends, I prayed even more.

My son, Ethan, is an Eagle Scout. He has phenomenal outdoor skills and has training to be a great leader. As a young man, he *now* has very good judgment. This was not always so. As Will Rogers said, "Good judgment comes from experience. Experience comes from poor judgment." Ethan had his opportunity to exercise poor judgment in the safe environment of a scout troop. And most boy scout troops end up backpacking sometime during their career. Whenever we hiked, he always liked to be in front. When he was younger, he was like a jack rabbit sprinting out ahead. But, being shorter then, he failed to look up above his eye level to follow the trail blazes and followed the foot-worn trail instead. He was not unusual, most of the boys did the same thing when they were at the point. There were many Boy Scout hikes that included a couple of occasions of doubling back to find the trail when a young scout was at the point. This time we were not in the safe environment of a Boy Scout hike; we were in the bottom of the Grand Canyon and several days' walk – at best – from help.

One afternoon on the Escalante Route was particularly memorable. The boys followed one another and I lagged behind. The trail went up and around an enormous boulder, about the size of a house. But another path went straight and flat under the boulder that overlooked an 800 foot drop. The boys followed the well-worn path right to the edge of the cliff and had to practically crawl on a two foot wide outcropping to squeeze themselves and their packs under the boulder. They didn't see the safer, but slightly more strenuous, marked trail. After being scared almost to death, I immediately had a talk with the boys about the necessity of following the cairns. The cairns marked the safe route, while seemingly obvious "trails" could lead to serious injury or death.

I told them the next critical turn was not obvious. They had to *look* for the cairns. The trail followed a ledge along a side canyon but only about half way. Other hikers had worn another path that went straight and seemed safe at first: however, it led to dangerous cliffs with slippery footings worse than what we had just passed through. They had to look for a rock slide that looked dangerous, but was in reality quite safe. It was marked by cairns *down* into a slot canyon. They had to *search* for the cairns.

Again, they dutifully followed the leader. They marched around the corner and into the side canyon following the trail as it meandered about half way up the canyon wall on a rock ledge. Being older and tired, I took things slower that day. As I came around the corner, I saw they were about a quarter of a mile past the cairn marking the route. I yelled at them to come back. But all the boys argued with me, telling me they were on the trail, the path was obvious, and there was no offshoot. They were sure they were on the right path. I stayed put and made them come back to me. I told them to look. They saw nothing. I told them to look again. Then one of the boys saw it. A cairn half way down a rockslide that looked impassible. Then they argued that it was impossible for such a steep way to be the trail and that they could not possibly go down there. I told them that although it did not look it, this way was safer than where they were going and led to a wonderland of a sandstone slot canyon. One by one they picked their way down, and found it was much easier than it looked. With a five foot drop to a sandy floor, we left the barren desert cliff and were in a cool, shadowy maze of sandstone. Red and orange horizontal stripes seemed to ooze around boulders washed down by floods. Where it could be seen, the sky was only a periwinkle ribbon twisting directly above. This natural cathedral awed us. This path lead us directly to the Colorado River: water and rest.

People get lost and die in the Grand Canyon every year. The National Park Service does everything it can to keep people from getting lost and dying by maintaining trails and educating visitors. But, the sojourners themselves are ultimately responsible for finding their way to safety. The cairns are there, but each hiker must search for them for himself or herself. There are many paths that lead away from safety to death. If you follow your own sensibilities and not those who have marked the one safe way, you put yourself in peril unnecessarily. If you follow others blindly and dutifully, you will certainly be in danger. If you follow your own sensibilities, you will get lost. "It is not within man who walks to direct his steps."

God's Path and Men's Paths. The paths that we are treading in life should be those blazed by Christ and His apostles at the direction of the Holy Spirit. God has laid out the path where we should walk. "Set up road signs; put up guideposts. Take note of the highway, the road that you take." Jeremiah 31:22. But over the centuries, many different trails have come up that criss-cross *the* way and tease us off the real path. The side trails never lead us to our destination. But, with the path being marked, how could anyone get off? Many of us do get off the trail every day. We are often too concerned about following *a* trail that we fail to look the cairns that mark *the* trail to our destination. We often follow others walking ahead of us and not the Way. We fail to diligently search for the way that we should walk.

Over the past many centuries many men and women have set out on bold treks with a single, lofty destination: they wanted to find the original trail marked by Christ. They decided to "reform" an existing church or to "restore" the Church of the New Testament. They did not want to just fix what existed; they wanted to go back to the original. These people wanted a faith that was based on scripture and wanted to reject everything else. These believers tried hard to set things right. They created the heritage of faith that has been passed to us today. Many strive to follow in their footsteps. But, an old Apache teacher said, "It is not enough for us just to walk in the paths of our fathers; we must seek the destinations that they sought."

The forefathers did the best they could to follow the scriptures only. Trying to rediscover the original ways, they put together things based on their perceptions and prior practices. Their cobbled practices unwittingly became a pattern for worship that has stood for decades. For many, those practices have become the only path to follow, having turned into written creeds, or worse, a *de facto* creed. These creeds have been established through actual statements of faith, creeds and catechisms. Even more subtly, groups who shun creeds have still established creeds through colleges, lesson books, commentaries and gospel magazines. It has been established by word of mouth and group practices. (It is ironic that the first point of several groups' creeds is that they do not have a creed!) As a result, many sincere brothers and sisters tend to follow the old practices or creeds but do not the search the scriptures themselves. Following a creed is like following a trail without looking for cairns, the marked path. The walker is following a trail of some kind, but not necessarily *the* trail marked by Christ.

Creed-following manifests itself in subtle ways. For example, many have learned the creed "don't use musical instruments" when singing religious songs. In reality, the scriptures tell us to *speak* to one another in psalms, hymns and spiritual songs. Ephesians 5:19. Creed-following has lead some to accompany themselves with humming or vocal noises simulating musical instruments while others sing words. By making nonsense noises, they are not "speaking to one another," but they are abiding by the creed: "don't use musical instruments." Apparently they do not realize that speaking like a gong or a cymbal has no worth. 1 Corinthians 13:1.

One serious problem with these creeds is that many of the conclusions are not wrong – at least to our current understanding – which is probably more insidious. It is more insidious because it draws us to follow the creeds and not the scriptures. However, if we merely copy what they did, we are not following the scriptures. One scholar noted that back-to-the-Bible movements that shun creeds last only about three generations. The first two generations focus on the scriptures. The third generation tends to follow the conclusions of the prior two generations and a new denomination or sect is born. As in the words of the Roman Catholic hymn many often sing, "Faith of our fathers, holy faith! We will be true to thee[2] till death." Too often we are following our forefathers without realizing it. If our forefathers happened to have followed a rabbit trail, then we are following a rabbit trail as well. It is up to each of us to find *the* trail. It is up to each of us to check the cairns to make sure that we are following the right path. Otherwise, we will look up one day and realize we are on the edge of the cliff. Or worse, we might stubbornly insist that the group we are following is right and will find out too late that we were all wrong.

Dangers of Leaving the Path. Basing your path on God's trail markers is critical; basing our worship on God's revealed plan is essential. God has demonstrated His demand for our strict compliance with the law regulating how we should revere Him.

Nadab and Abihu were sons of Aaron, the first High Priest, and the nephews of Moses. At the beginning of worship under the Law, these men held a special place. When Moses went up to the mountain to receive the tablets of stone, God told him to bring Aaron, Nadab, Abihu and the seventy elders to come to the base of the mountain to worship God from afar. God even allowed these men to "see" Him. God appointed them as priests.

---

[2] The word "thee" here refers to the "fathers" in "Faith of our Fathers" and not God in this hymn. Frederick W. Faber, who converted to Catholicism six years before he wrote this hymn, was very careful in his capitalization.

Exodus 28:1 and 29:9 They witnessed the inauguration of the worship in the tabernacle when fire came out of Heaven: Lev 9:1-2,22-24. The things they witnessed were awesome in every sense of the word. So why did Nadab and Abihu offer "unauthorized fire" to God? Leviticus 10. (NIV) The knew which fire they were to use. They had witnessed the fire being given. However, they treated God's things carelessly, and God killed them – meaningfully – with fire from heaven. When they were killed, God warned Moses and Aaron: "By those who come near Me I will be treated as holy, And before all the people I will be honored." Leviticus 10:3. Even these men, who were chosen by God, who saw a vision of God, who witnessed God's power and glory, approached God casually. They failed to follow the trail that had been marked for them. If we are approaching God in *worship*, we must approach Him in the way He has said.

David was a man also chosen by God. However, David failed to treat the things pertaining to the worship of God – and, therefore, God Himself – as holy. He was tricked into following a side-trail. Before there was a king in Israel, the nation fought with the Philistines. Because the Israelites were afraid of losing, they brought out the Ark of the Covenant, treating it almost as if it were a sort of good luck charm or secret weapon. They were treating holy things trivially. The Philistines ultimately captured the Ark. But God punished the Philistines because of it, and the Philistines sought to get rid of the ark. The Philistine priests determined to send the ark back on a cart pulled by two cows that had just given birth. 1 Samuel 6:7-9. God led the cows contrary to their nature to remain with their calves and returned the ark to Israel. But, the priests of Dagon chose methods that were contrary to the Law. Many years later, when David needed to move the Ark from one place to another, he went back to history, to the old paths, to determine how to do it. He built a cart.

Moving the ark on a cart was the way it was done previously. That is how it had been done before. That "must" be the way it should be moved now. But, there was a clear method of transporting the ark prescribed by the scriptures: the priests were to carry the ark. See Exodus 25 and Numbers 4. When one of the oxen pulling the cart stumbled, Uzzah touched the ark to steady it. "The Lord's anger burned against Uzzah because of his irreverent act; therefore, God struck him down and he died there beside the ark of God." 2 Samuel 6:7. What was David's reaction? Anger and fear! Even after the death of Uzzah, David apparently did not realize that he had sinned in how *he* had treated the holy things of God. Without realizing it, David had followed a trail marked by men and not by God.

We also know that adding things to worship beyond what is commanded is also condemned. Jeroboam was chastised for having instituted a new feast day on the fifteenth day of the eighth month. 1 Kings 12:33. He just added a new day: he did not take away the others. It would be a good thing to worship God more, right? No, Jeroboam made a new path that had not been marked by God.

No Cairns. There are places in the Grand Canyon where the soil is alive. Cryptobiotic soil forms a delicate crust of lichen on the desert surface. It is so delicate and fragile that a single footprint will destroy that patch for one hundred years. The only way to preserve it is to not touch it in any way. So when a trail leads through a plateau with this type of vegetation on the ground, you stay on the path. How do you stay on the path? The answer sounds silly: you do not go where the path is not. One sure way to know where the path is not, is the absence of cairns along the way. Hikers know that they should not go a certain way because the rangers did not mark that way as a path. If they stray, they run into the possibility of doing irreparable damage, becoming lost, or dying. In the same way, God has marked our path. If we see no markers, it is a pretty good sign that we have wandered far off the path. What do we do when we see no cairns? Are we free to wander at will? How should we treat the silence of the scriptures? Are we free to do whatever we want?

Right now, most of us are like boys ambling along failing to realize that our "trail" has no markers. Being confident in our path, our leaders, and ourselves, we fail to realize we are walking down a path without *searching* for the markers laid out by God. Because we think we already know the way, we fail to seek God's way. As an elder in a congregation once told me, "I don't need three lessons on [a certain scripture]. I've read it. I've studied it. And, I don't need any more lessons on it." Without looking and looking again to scripture for our authority, we are condemned to follow our own sensibilities or to follow someone other than God. We may be walking in the paths of our fathers; but we are not seeking the destinations they sought.

If you are following paths that are marked by traditions, creeds and teachings of a particular group, you may not be following the path that God laid our for us. Commonly, "second and third generation" Christians have difficulty distinguishing between the teachings of their heritage and God's paths.

2: THE CHURCH DRUG

If you are reading this book, I hope it is because you are searching. Either you're looking for something missing in your Church-life or you might be looking for something to add to your Church life. You might be looking for more ways to grow. You might be wondering why your Church isn't growing as it should. Why are people leaving your Church? There are countless studies why this is so: I do not have the answers. However, you are searching for those markers that direct you to Life. Jesus came to give us Life and Life abundantly. John 10:10. We have looked for those cairns marking the path to Life in, to, around and through the Church.

So many times I've heard Christians explain how wonderful a Church service was because of the sermon delivered or because of the music. A good Church is one where the preacher or pastor has a flair for words and moving delivery, giving Christians an inoculation from sin for at least another seven days. For others the search seems satisfied by an uplifting message or emotional appeal. Some people look for programs either for their youth or themselves. Therefore, numbers increase, both in attendance and in income.

A "good" Church is one that has good classes and programs for "people of all ages." Some parents Church-shop until they find one that offers enough programs for children. I met one man who went to a Church so he could play on their baseball team. One older woman was attached to her Church because it had a social club for older people during the week. One woman prided herself by being on the flower committee, providing floral arrangements around the building every Sunday morning.

Some are drawn to a Church by its music. Because of different tastes, Christians are involved in worship controversies. Do we stick with the old songs? Do the new songs move us more? The vibrato of an organ echoing along with a choir moves some. A capella singing in mass numbers moves others. A solo violinist playing the tune for "Amazing Grace" may move some to tears. Young people sitting around a campfire singing can evoke that emotional "kumbaya" feeling. No matter who you are – conservative, liberal, denominational, independent, instrumental, a capella, a worship leader, or a praise singer – you may be looking for that certain feeling when you assemble with other Christians. You may even be so conservative that you are stifling any emotionality in a worship service, intentionally seeking a Church that *doesn't* move you emotionally.

No matter where you search in a Church, the problem – your search – is unsolvable. Rachel Held Evans, a popular blogger on religion, wrote,

> Time and again, the assumption among Christian leaders, and evangelical leaders in particular, is that the key to drawing twenty-somethings back to church is simply to make a few style updates – edgier music, more casual services, a coffee shop in the fellowship hall, a pastor who wears skinny jeans, an updated Web site that includes online giving. But here's the thing: Having been advertised to our whole lives, we millennials have highly sensitive BS meters, and we're not easily impressed with consumerism or performances. In fact, I would argue that church-as-performance is just one more thing driving us away from the church, and evangelicalism in particular.[3]

Looking to update Church services or to base worship on humanly attractive things, is not the answer.

I have a good friend who became addicted to opiates, first, through drugs prescribed by a doctor. Then as he became addicted, he acquired them illegally. When he first started taking the drugs, just a little affected him in a big way. Eventually he needed more and more to get the same level of "high." He told me that just before he quit, he had to take such high levels that they nearly killed him. He knew people had died taking opiates at the levels he was taking. This is usually how people addicted to opiates die: they need to take such high levels to reach a certain level of intoxication – because their tolerance level increases with continued use – until the level they need to be intoxicated coincides with the amount that stops their bodily

3 Rachel Held Evans, "Why millennials are leaving the church," CNN Belief Blog. http://religion.blogs.cnn.com/2013/07/27/why-millennials-are-leaving-the-church/

functions. The dilemma is unsolvable: unsolvable unless one quits taking the drug. There is no cure other than withdrawal.

Similar things happen with Church. Unfortunately, there is no cure. Three things happen with Churches: they become emotionless places, they become unchanging places, or they become places of intellectual snobbery and ignorance perpetuation.

The unfeeling Church. Some are convinced there is not supposed to be an emotional feeling or deep connection in Church. So when it's not there, we don't miss it. On the other hand, we are so used to shallow Church relationships we think that's all there is. How many times is a person asked on a Sunday morning, "How are you doing?" They may say terrible. "I'll pray for you this week" is the response. The same question is asked the next Sunday with the same answer. Nothing happens week after week. Peggy Lee's heartbreaking song from 1969 sums up how many people feel about their Church: "If that's all there is my friends, then let's keep dancing." They believe their Church is right, so regardless of how it feels or how little our fellow Christians help us, "let's keep dancing." All that Church gives us is guilt for feeling a numbness to our very real spiritual pain. With no relief for our spiritual pain, many leave. Others may stay because "that's all there is my friends."

Self-imposed abulia. "Abulia" is a psychological term where one is incapable of or lacks the capability to make decisions independently. We keep reaching and reaching for a new level of "high," and we don't find it within our "faith." So we reach a spiritual numbness unable to "legally" get a new high and are disappointed: so we frustratingly "plateau" so to speak. This puts us in a psychological dilemma. To remain true to our core values (whether expressed in a written or unwritten creed), we are prohibited from seeking religious experiences that we think will satisfy us when they happen be outside our Church's core beliefs. So rather than abandon our creeds, we stay put making no decision to improve our status because to make an improvement involves change, and change involves risk. We do nothing but stagnate. On the other hand, our indecision makes us frustrated, and we give up: we leave the Church. Or, we stay in our Church and become the living dead–neither hot nor cold.

Craving the next high. There are two kinds of highs that are contrary to each other but are equally fatal: emotional fixes and intellectual fixes.

Emotional junkies. One is a quest for emotional experiences. We seek a higher and higher emotional fix with each "religious" experience. This is well documented throughout the centuries. Isaac Watts was disaffected singing the Psalms, so he wrote his own songs. The Wesleys realized the deadness of traditional Protestantism, so they created Methodism in the eighteenth century. D. L. Moody saw the need for an emotional plea in his ministry, so Ira Sankey and Fanny J. Crosby flooded the nineteenth century church with new songs. This isn't an exaggeration: Crosby wrote over 8000 hymns! Sankey toured with Moody for many years inventing and promoting the emotionalism of the altar call that persists to this day. Then the twentieth century saw the peppy Stamps-Baxter style of music become the standard. The latter part of the twentieth century exploded with new songs, new words, non-traditional worship services, and Broadway type shows: all attempted to satisfy a longing for the next new "high." Church services of folk music competed with tradition and then became Church services of rock-inspired hymns. I remember one woman in the 1970s expressing how much she loved the folk song "Blowing in the Wind" because it was sung in her Church's folk service. Now in the twenty-first century, recording artists turn their messages into multimedia events. I've head Christians effervesce with excitement over Christian performances. Some of these are excellent productions. However great each performance may be, eventually each one will become an opiate high that will intersect the point where we flat-line. Again we will be dead or struggling with a lethally high dose of emotionalism. Still more people experiment with house Churches hoping something magical will appear while meeting away from a traditional Church. However, one of two things happen: we leave the Church unsatisfied, seeking out that next greater emotional boost or high. Or, worse, we turn back: back into burned-out, emotionless zombies, giving up believing that such emotional satisfaction or fulfillment exists and return to the status quo or worse. Many just give up.

Intellectual junkies: Dealers and addicts. The second type of high has been deeply embedded within the Church for millennia: intellectualism.[4] It, too, has a fatal opiate-high crash. Since Constantine (who reigned from 306 to 337) injected the concept of clergy into the Church, there arose a

---

[4] Please understand, I am not against study and attaining knowledge.

separation that never existed in God's plan. Throughout the New Testament there was never a clergy-layman distinction. Speaking of the New Covenant, Jeremiah said, "And they shall teach no more every man his neighbor, and every man his brother, saying, Know the Lord: for they shall all know me, from the least of them unto the greatest of them, saith the Lord...." Jeremiah 31:34. Contrary to what God said, if clergy or priests exist, it would seem natural that they must necessarily have some special training or education above everyone else. Historically, priest training became the norm. Following the Reformation, priest-training became pastor-training, and seminaries sprouted up all sanctioned by and supported by the Church. Now, pastor training has become preacher training in other groups. Even movements that claim to be independent of traditional denominations consider colleges for preachers to be essential or desirable for the Church to progress. For example Alexander Campbell, who was trying to restore "first century Christianity" in the early nineteenth century, believed a college was necessary for the success of what is known as the Stone-Campbell movement: he started Bethany College in Bethany, Virginia. Speaking in slightly exaggerated terms, to be a preacher or pastor, one needs special training or special knowledge to pass that special knowledge on to those who don't have such knowledge. A two-level class system has developed. However, that opiate of the quest for higher knowledge kills from both sides of the pulpit.

First, the continual quest to gain a full understanding of the unknowable God drives many scholars to distraction. Clergy study Greek and Hebrew. They study hermeneutics, theology, etymology, eschatology, sociology: just about every -ology but scatology.[5] There is no end to the quest for knowledge: "But beyond this, my son, be warned: the writing of many books is endless, and excessive devotion to books is wearying to the body." Ecclesiastes 12:12. The elusive pursuit of human explanations of the divine teases pastors, clergy or preachers along. (For purposes here we will refer to them as "clergy.") They attend seminars, lectureships, continuing education, or just that one more degree. Much of this learning is aimed at learning many other and often conflicting theologies: learning what is not is emphasized over learning what is. There is more time studying human

---

[5] I wouldn't be surprised if scatology showed up as a course in some seminary somewhere.

philosophies and little time simply letting God's word become part of themselves. They believe to truly strengthen the Church the clergy must chase the unattainable or reach a false perception in their competition with others that they've reach a level of respect. That way they can disseminate their great knowledge, and the common members can glean from them.

This also sets up the opposite addiction among the "regular," lay members, which usually includes the elders or other leaders of the Church. The men and women sitting in the pew hearing an eloquent sermon can't spend the days cloistered in a study coming up with great thoughts, pithy language and great quotes. Therefore, Christians feel that their individual understanding of the scriptures is inadequate, and they become dependent on a high-powered, Bible injection they receive on Sunday mornings. After all, the preacher went to school to learn all this that he's telling us; we didn't go to college to learn so much about the Bible. Therefore, the less-than-clergy, common Christians give up on feeding themselves from the Word of God and become dependent on a regular sermon-fix from an "expert." Food prepared by a trained chef is always better than home-cooking, right? Or, a microwave dinner is quicker and less messy than if I have to put all the components together myself. The clergy then have a weekly challenge. Each week's sermon must continually be new, fresh and interesting; otherwise the preacher gets fired for a better speaker or the members find another Church with better "cuisine." Or worse, they succumb to the inertia of numbness and no one can tell whether the Church is alive or dead.

This attitude creates a self-destructive, symbiotic addiction: common members need the clergy to teach them some "special knowledge;" while clergy need an audience to support them while they dispense their "special knowledge." The laymen don't want to give up on the idea of a preacher or pastor, because that would mean that they would have to study on their own, and they can never reach the pinnacles of knowledge on which the clergy perch. The clergy cannot argue against their own existence as part of the Church. They've been taught that they are essential to it: many are the *de facto* CEO's of their Church. Plus, they can't consider a clergy-less church because they would be leaving a flock leaderless and, more importantly, they would be out of a job. It is a self-perpetuating whirlpool, sucking innumerable clergy and laymen into oblivion. It would seem that we are in a dilemma. Christians must be in a Church, but they are emotionless, unchanging, intellectual places. Or the Church is a thrill ride of emotions, a source of uplifting entertainment, or a weekly symposium for the intelligentsia. Or some harrowing combination of these. Whether emotional, entertaining or enlightening, Church doesn't make us better Christians.

What if? At this point I want to insert a radical idea. What if "the Church" doesn't really exist at all? What if the Church as it has existed for centuries was never part of God's plan? What if that institution that we devote our lives to and that many have died for, never really existed at all? If this is true, we wouldn't be seeking our next emotional fix. If this is true, we wouldn't be feeling numb and unfulfilled. If this is true, we wouldn't be using religion as an opiate for ourselves, much less for "the masses."[6]

Meanings change. Words change in meaning over time. If I tell a man he is a "nice person," I'd be thanked for the complement. If I told a man that he was a "nice person" five hundred years ago, I'd probably get punched in the face.[7] When Frank Sinatra sang the words, "Just for now, let's call it romance, just for now, let's take a chance... Just for now, let's not be clever, just for now, let's just be gay...", he was not talking about having a homosexual relationship with a member of the Rat Pack. Meanings change.

The meaning of word *church* also has changed over time, too. Just how the word *church* came into English takes considerable study: an entire page of the Oxford English Dictionary is devoted to this topic. In summary, *church* comes from an Old English word which meant a building, usually a palatial one. With the cross-evangelistic efforts around the fourth and fifth centuries, the Old English and West German terms generally merged into the word *kirke*, which eventually became in English, *church*. Arising from the Roman Catholic efforts, the modern English word *church* is a commingling of human ideas. Starting as a palatial building, *church* came to mean a building dedicated to the public worship of God, or the public place of worship of any religion. Because how the specialized word *church* came into English, it also now means "a particular, organized Christian society, considered as the only true representative, or as distinct branch of the Church universal, separated by doctrine, worship, organization, or confined to limits territorial

---

[6] The phrase, "Religion is the opiate of the masses" has been aptly used by Marquis de Sade (1797), Novalis (1798), Karl Marx (1844), and Charles Kingsley (1847). Ironically, Madeline Murray O'Hare said that the opiate of the masses was baseball.

[7] Five hundred years ago, *nice* meant foolish or stupid.

or historical."[8] In English, then, we bypassed the entire idea of *ekklesia* and went straight to Constantine's organizational structure, the construction of buildings, manufactured hierarchies, defined worship and created man-made creeds.[9]

By the fifth century, *church* included a building, a pastor, priest or parson, a structured Church service, and an institutional organization. All of these historical concepts have stayed embedded in English speakers' meaning of *church*. Church reformers, restorers and rebuilders have all retained one or more of the appendages that have been grafted onto the Church. The idea of *ekklesia* in the English language has never existed in the word *Church*.[10]

Where from here? Many Christians live in a "Churchless" environment that is more stimulating, and more spiritually satisfying than anything a Churchgoer could possibly imagine: they belong to an *ekklesia.* You may be surprised that many people – even "strong" Christians – equate "going to Church" to having a vampire plunge his fangs into their carotid arteries, sucking the very life from their beings. Many will be flabbergasted, flummoxed or furious at the very thought that abundant life – the abundant life that only Christ gives – comes from outside the institution known as the Church.

Now here is a caution. You may not see a problem. If you do not see a problem, you may not have one or you may just not realize it yet. Many Christians are very pleased with their religious experiences. If you're one of those people, don't read any farther. First, I am writing this book to bring richness to people's lives who are not finding it in other places. Second, I do not want to cause division or contention: I want unity. God does not allow me to judge the hearts and minds of fellow believers. If you are content, I am happy for you. When you sing Psalm 42, "So my soul pants for You, O God. My soul thirsts for God, for the living God," I hope you have a rumbling of hunger in the pit of your soul. If you do decide to read on, I pray that your

---

[8] *The Compact Edition of the Oxford English Dictionary, Volume 1*, page 411.

[9] *Pagan Christianity*, by Frank Viola, contains a detailed description of how "the church" got to where it is today.

[10] In 1536, Tyndale translated the word *ekklesia* as *congregation* rather than *church*. The translation was banned and most copies were burned so Tyndale's influence of the translation of *ekklesia* is limited.

life – your *real* spiritual life – will be enriched beyond your wildest imagination. It will be enriched in ways that can only come from the mind and plan of God.

The *ekklesia* is not a place or a building. The *ekklesia* is not based on a system of human thought or theology. The *ekklesia* is not an organization to make you feel better or to guilt you into staying a member. The *ekklesia* is probably not what you think of as a Church.

3: SEEING WHAT IS NOT.
OVERLOOKING WHAT IS.

For centuries God's creatures existed in people's minds as legend and myth. Stories of mythical giant squids were terror-tales of ancient sailors for centuries until live specimens were photographed in the twenty-first century. When Europeans first reported the "discovery" of the platypus, many European scientists considered the reports of an egg-laying mammal fraudulent. When people encounter something they are unfamiliar with, disbelief or distrust is usually their first reaction. The reaction is quite natural. We see things only as we expect to see them. We expect to see things in harmony with our experiences.

However, human skepticism works in the opposite way as well. Some people treasure falsehoods even when the truth is obvious. Charlie Chaplin came in third place in a Charlie Chaplin look-alike contest. The Flat Earth Society is still alive and kicking.[11]

Some "facts" are really misunderstandings: if I were asked who was the first person to circumnavigate the earth, I'd probably answer Ferdinand Magellan. I'd be wrong: he never made it, dying in the Philippines before he could finish his trip. It is commonly taught that Guglielmo Marconi invented the radio. He did not: it was Nikola Tesla.[12] Still, the "fact" appears in most text books. Then there are lies that are just commonly accepted as fact. For example, "all" Americans know that Abner Doubleday invented baseball in Cooperstown, Ohio in 1839 – that is a complete, utter and deliberate fabrication.

Getting what you expect. Accompanying our belief and knowledge systems is an inherent flaw: if we perceive or understand a thing in a certain way, we will receive whatever it is in harmony with our perceptions and

---

[11] theflatearthsociety.org

[12] Marconi Wireless Tel. Co. v. United States, 1943, 320 U.S. 1

beliefs. We have self-fulfilling "prophecies" that reinforce our own falsehoods. I may think a certain food tastes bad and chances are I will not like it if given the chance to taste it. My little dog barks when someone walks in front of my house. Eventually they keep walking on. In her little mind, the person left because she barked so ferociously. She barks more the next day because she thought it worked before! A server at a restaurant may see a sloppily dressed patron and presume that he's a bad tipper. The patron detects the attitude and becomes a bad patron. He gets bad service. The server gets a bad tip. Everyone receives what they expected and their expectations are confirmed. In other words, we frequently confirm our own misunderstandings.

Our minds are also wired to see things according to patterns we already have. When we receive information, we stash it away in mental boxes that we have established based upon our experiences. Pareidolia is the phenomenon in which we see faces in random objects or patterns. Our minds are conditioned from birth to recognize patterns based on prior experiences. When a new idea or concept is presented, our minds try to make it fit within the mental boxes we already have. Sometimes our boxes are full of lies or misunderstandings or are improperly arranged; therefore, a new truth is rejected or misunderstood because it doesn't fit with what we already "know."

Hostility toward change. Civility and open-mindedness foster genuine quests for truth, but they rarely coexist among humanity in general and, unfortunately, among Christians even more rarely. Snarking barbs in blogs and religious discussions is more the norm than the exception. Fear of being wrong or fear of losing face – among other fears – thwart honest searches. Solomon said, "Do not associate with a man *given* to anger; or go with a hot-tempered man, or you will learn his ways and find a snare for yourself." Proverbs 22:24-26. John said, "A real love for others will chase those worries away. The thought of being punished is what makes us afraid. It shows that we have not really learned to love." 1 John 4:18 (CEV). New Age spiritualist Marianne Williamson put it another way, "We are so trained in the thought system of fear and attack that we get to the point where natural thinking – love – feels unnatural and unnatural thinking – fear – feels natural. It takes real discipline and training to unlearn the thought system of fear." She is right: fear keeps us from learning.[13] Henry David Thoreau said,

---

[13] Scripturally Williamson has this backwards: fear is our natural state; love is our unnatural, or spiritual, state.

"When any real progress is made, we unlearn and learn anew what we thought we knew before." Or, as Paul put it, "Therefore let him who thinks he stands take heed that he does not fall." 1 Corinthians 10:12. If you think you understand something well, you probably don't.

Translators sometimes obscure meanings. One of the largest disservices to Christians has been translators helping people "understand" the scriptures by refusing to translate words. Instead, they made up English words based upon the original Greek word. The New Testament uses very few terms that were strictly religious; however, the translators inserted or created religious terms to justify or buttress a certain religious system, creed, or thought. Where perfectly good English words existed, religiously charged words were inserted into their place.

Dipping and Baptizing. Take for example the word *baptize*. For over four hundred years no Christian in England was baptized; Christians were "dipped." The word *baptize* came across the English Channel with the French invasion in 1066. Wycliffe used the "more sophisticated" French derived word when he translated the scriptures between 1382 and 1395. English words were looked down upon as common and French-derived words were sophisticated.[14] Even after Wycliffe, the words *dip* and *baptize* coexisted until the Authorized or King James translation appeared in 1611. "King James" killed the common English word until we were left with a religious word that hides the real meaning of the Greek's *baptizo*. In English, we are dipped no more.

Apostles and Sent Messengers. Another example is the word *apostle*. In Greek, the word is *apostolos* which means "a messenger" or "one who is sent." So rather than use the term "messenger," the translators mystified it on most occasions by substituting an English-styled Greek work. It's interesting that the King James translators used the word *messenger* when the context was clearly not referring to one of "the twelve": Phillippians 2:25 and 2 Corinthians 8:23. But when *apostolos* is used in Ephesians 4:11, the translator spin didn't grant some to be "messengers" but spun them into "Apostles." You might think that inventing new religious words isn't really that big of a deal; but it is. Making "Apostle" a religious word, hides the meaning when talking about sending someone to be a messenger of the

---

[14] Think about it: we eat beef and pork– French words – but not cows and pigs – English words.

gospel. If "apostle" were a verb in English, think about how much more powerful these words of God would be:

- Matthew 10:5-6: "Jesus *apostled* these twelve out, and commanded them, saying, "Don't go among the Gentiles, and don't enter into any city of the Samaritans. Rather, go to the lost sheep of the house of Israel."
- Matthew 14:35-36: "When the people of that place recognized him, they *apostled* into all that surrounding region, and brought to him all who were sick, and they begged him that they might just touch the fringe of his garment. As many as touched it were made whole."
- Romans 10:14-15: "How then will they call on him in whom they have not believed? How will they believe in him whom they have not heard? How will they hear without a preacher? And how will they preach unless they are *apostled*?

On the other hand, what if we just used the English term we already had? *Messengers*. We wouldn't be so mixed up when we read that Jesus is called "the Messenger and High Priest of our confession." Hebrews 3:1. And we wouldn't be so confused when Paul talks about Andronicus and Junia – Junia being a woman – who are "notable among the messengers." Romans 16:7.

Now, demystifying the term *apostle* layers on some stunningly intense ramifications for us as Christians. Remember the beautiful picture of the church with Jesus, the Chief cornerstone – "the Messenger...of our confession" – and its foundation of the "Apostles/Messengers, the foundation stones of precious gems? "The wall of the city had twelve foundations, and on them twelve names of the twelve Apostles of the Lamb." Revelation 21:14. As Christ is the Messenger-Cornerstone and the Apostles are the Messenger-Foundation stones, our faith is built upon and based upon the message they gave us. This really gives us a different perspective on their role as part of that spiritual building.

So, instead of using "messenger" or "person sent," we end up with a sanctified, glorified term, a*postle*, which splotches blotches of religious iconography on God's simple words. Occasionally, the real color of the meaning shines through if we scrape off a few layers.

The real focus: the *ekklesia*. So many everyday Greek words have been elevated, exalted and sanctified that they could fill up a book – but definitely not this book. The Light is dimmer each time a plain Greek word gets covered by an English religious bushel. It is a shame that translators avoid plain words that could otherwise make the scriptures shine brighter. If we take the bushel off of the common Greek word *ekklesia*, it will shine. Perhaps its brightness can even overpower the term *church*.

My hope in this little chapter is twofold. First, I hope that you, as the reader, can get past your prejudices. I hope I can get past mine, too. It is so difficult to look at familiar things through fresh eyes. We live in a world where we tend to accept things as they are presented to us. Marshall McLuhan observed, "Everybody experiences far more than he understands. Yet it is experience, rather than understanding, that influences behavior." It is our experience with "The Church" that makes us *think* that we understand the *ekklesia*. In reality, our *experiences* – good or bad – give us our understanding of "The Church," even if that understanding may be dead wrong. Second, I hope to create in you the wonder of your first visit as a child to Disneyland or the Magic Kingdom (or some other fantastic place) and translating that wonder into wandering around and wondering at the City of God: His *ekklesia*. Ezekiel and John spend so much time describing how wonderful the *ekklesia* is that we tend to consider it hyperbole: in these instances God is NOT exaggerating. In fact, I believe that God is holding back.

Let me point out my own hypocrisy with a purpose. Throughout the beginning chapters, *Church* will refer to what man has constructed or to describe where we are today. I will use the word *ekklesia* to refer to what God is talking about in the scriptures. Once we examine God's *ekklesia*, perhaps we can come up with an English word that conveys the meaning behind *ekklesia* rather than hide it in the term *Church* with all the false meanings and traditions we have crammed into and plastered over it.

With boldness, let us begin to look. Glimpsing the fantastic creation of God, the *ekklesia*, might just give us a bit of the wonder that those scientists experienced when they first saw the mythical giant squid, alive and swimming. Seeing the pinnacle of creation, the living, breathing *ekklesia*, will trivialize centuries of man's misconceptions.

However, before we can see the entire forest, we must first be able to see a tree. As we see one tree, and then another tree, we can see the qualities of each and how they are interconnected. Before we can understand the *ekklesia*, we must first understand the individuals that constitute it and how they interrelate.

An *ekklesia* may be very different from our experiences with a Church of just Church in general. The real meaning of *ekklesia* is better understood by looking at it objectively rather than through the lens of Church history or our own experiences with Church.

TOM MANN

PART TWO: PERSONAL IDENTITY

TOM MANN

4: BELIEVING YOU ARE SOMETHING ELSE

Dove, the maker of hair and skin care products, conducted an experiment. They selected a group of women and then introduced them to total strangers. They paired one of the strangers with one of the women and asked the stranger to become acquainted with that woman. Next, the women met with a forensic artist individually. He could not see their faces. He asked them questions to describe themselves, and he drew them according to their own descriptions. When the sketch was completed, the women would leave unseen by the artist. Then, the strangers came in, one-by-one, and described the woman assigned to him or her. The forensic artist drew the picture of how the women were viewed by strangers. The sketches of the women were then placed side by side. Without fail, the strangers saw the women as more beautiful than the women saw themselves.[15] The women tended to focus on negative things about themselves: they felt too fat, their mothers told them their chins were too big, or they emphasized moles or scars. Sadly, Christians view themselves in a similar way.

Recently, a Sunday school class of young people was asked a simple, but baffling, question: "Who are you?" Most of these young adults had been attending Church, Sunday School and Bible classes since they were babies. Their answers were almost consistently negative. They saw themselves as unforgiven sinners. They saw their imperfections. They dwelt on their weaknesses as humans. They said they were incapable of being "good enough." They felt they hadn't done enough to be forgiven. They felt undeserving of God's love. If an artist drew spiritual portraits as they saw themselves, the portraits would not be pretty.

Too often the Church emphasizes a negative trait or something wrong about ourselves. Guilt is used to keep members of the Church in line. Some

---

[15] http://realbeautysketches.dove.us/, retrieved April 19, 2013.

emphasize doing good deeds, even while acknowledging that we are saved by grace. Other Churches keep people in line by adherence to a creed, by the need to tithe, by regular attendance or by participation in a group, study or committee. Even many "feel good" Churches rely on some sort of hook to keep Church members attached. Even the peppy, entertaining worship services become that "thing" we need to forget our inadequacies and give us a six-day fix of spiritual anesthesia or numbness. Regardless, each Church-member will be a "slave" to the Church, to the organization. In the end, the conclusion will be "So you too, when you do all the things which are commanded you, say, 'We are unworthy slaves; we have done only that which we ought to have done.'" Luke 17:10.

Bundling and bungling. A major problem with Christians is they don't know who they are. Christians rely on a creed or confession for their identity. Many rely on their Church for their identity. "I'm a Catholic." "I'm a Lutheran." "I'm a Baptist." "I'm a member of the Christian Church." "I'm a member of the Church of Christ." It simplifies things. Membership in a Church or acceptance of a creed bundles beliefs and makes explaining things simpler.

A creed or confession, whether written or unwritten, is merely the bundle of theological ideas people have put together. My cable television service also comes with internet service and a landline telephone: I don't want a landline but it is "bundled" with the other services so I have no choice. Several years ago, I wanted to buy a new car with no extras: it came in basic silver, manual transmission, air conditioning and a radio/cassette tape player. When I asked if I could get a CD player, I was told I would have to get the next higher package that included all kinds of luxuries I didn't want. When I asked if I could get it in a different color, they said yes, but it would come with the custom trim package and power windows and cost $3000 more. I stuck with the cheap silver, no frills model. It is much the same with Churches: we get the whole package of their restatement or interpretation of the scriptures. To take in one idea is to take in them all. Or, we pick and choose among the bundles and find the one that is least objectionable, but those extra ideas that come with the package just keep the church-goer weighed down. No matter how well we restate things, we are always shy of the truth.

So when I try to find my identity through a Church or a Church's teaching, I will always find my self image filtered through their creeds and beliefs. Even those who claim to follow only the Bible have a common, unwritten understanding of what the Bible says. Inside a Church, we can only see ourselves through light that is filtered through centuries old stained glass or by the humming electric blue of florescent lights. We can only see ourselves when we look into the mirror, the perfect law of liberty. James 1. That is a churchless view.

Is identity important? I met a woman who had amnesia. She had been in an auto accident and afterward did not remember anything about her life. She did not know who she was. She did not know her children or her husband. She did not know her name. It was a frightening experience for her. She had to rely on others to tell her whom she was related to, where she lived and what her job was. When a person has amnesia, she is deprived of the knowledge of who she is. Most importantly, she is deprived of her relationships. She doesn't know where she fits in. She doesn't know where she belongs or who she can rely upon. She doesn't know who loves her. She may not know who or what is dangerous to her.

As spiritual beings, Satan does not want us to know who we are. Without knowing who we are, we do not know who we can rely upon, what has been done for us, where our home is, and, most importantly, who the enemy is. It is to Satan's advantage to keep a Christian's identity hidden or distorted in some way. When we see ourselves as impure sinners, we will be shackled with guilt. When we see ourselves as no different from the world, we lose our idea of being separate or "sanctified" for God. However, when we see ourselves as God sees us, then we can know our true identity. He is the only being who can be objective about our identity.

Whispering lies. Believing lies. During World War II, after the Nazis had invaded Poland, Heinrich Himmler implemented a devious plan. Polish children, some of whom were still babies, were kidnapped from their parents and placed in orphanages for children of unwed mothers. Older children were told their parents were dead. They were taught German and forbidden to speak Polish. Younger children forgot their parents. The children were given German names. They were given new birth certificates and new identities. The Nazis selected those with "desired" traits to be housed with German foster families or adopted outright. Through indoctrination, they came to believe that they were German, that these foster families were their real families and learned to hate the "inferior" Polish. After the war when some of the children were identified, many refused to believe they weren't German. Many were traumatized when they were removed from the family they thought was their own and returned to their Polish biological parents –

people who they didn't remember and who didn't speak their language. They had believed the lies told to them regarding their true identities.

Satan whispers lies about our identities, too.

Kidnapped from Christ. Satan has one tool. He uses lies. He lies because that is who he is. Jesus said, "He was a murderer from the beginning, and does not stand in the truth because there is no truth in him. Whenever he speaks a lie, he speaks from his own nature, for he is a liar and the father of lies." John 8:44. Jesus said "The thief comes only to steal and kill and destroy..." John 10:10. Or, as Peter described him, Satan is prowling "around like a roaring lion, seeking someone to devour." 1 Peter 5. With this limited arsenal, lies, it would seem that it would be easy to overcome these untruths. But, it is not that simple.

Satan is good at making his lies just *seem* right. He can disguise himself to appear as "an angel of light." 2 Corinthians 11:14. He "deceives the whole world." Revelation 12:9. Today, Christians can still be lured away and hardened by the "deceitfulness of sin." Hebrews 3:12-13. The Spirit warned that Christians would 'fall away from the faith, paying attention to deceitful spirits and doctrines of demons, by means of the hypocrisy of liars seared in their own conscience as with a branding iron...." 1 Timothy 4.

Jesus works in the opposite way. When Jesus was being questioned by Pilate, Jesus told the reason He had come into the world: "For this I have been born, and for this I have come into the world, to testify to the truth." John 18:37. John said that Jesus "appeared for this purpose, to destroy the works of the devil." 1 John 3:8. Jesus told Paul that his job was "to open their eyes so that they may turn from darkness to light and from the dominion of Satan to God...." Acts 26:18. Jesus works by flooding us with truth.

Every person operates from a belief system. We get these from all sorts of places: our parents, our siblings, our teachers, preachers, pastors, and our friends. They will make a comment or statement, and we will believe it and absorb that statement into ourselves even if it is untrue. These can be both "good" and "bad" lies. When we believe "good" lies, we will think we are beautiful or handsome, talented, intelligent, privileged or something else to inflate our ego. When we believe "bad" lies, we will believe ourselves to be wretched, sinful, unworthy, ugly, unloved, etc. It is as though we all have mental buckets of beliefs that have been filled with lies. Either way, these lies have been poured into us daily until they become part of the cloth of our personality. These lies can linger in our personality for our entire lifetimes unless we get rid of them.

If you watched the video that was referred to at the beginning of this chapter, one woman said, "My mother told me I had a big chin." She did not: but she believed that about herself, and it molded her self image. Satan pours lies into us more intensively as Christians. He brings up our failings, our sins, our shortcomings. He reminds us of how weak we are. He makes our cravings and lusts seem normal and that it is right and natural to satisfy them however we choose. Satan will make us feel like we have to work to make God love us. He makes us doubt our salvation. Or, he make us feel as though we've lost God's love because of something we've done or haven't done. He tells us we are alone and don't belong. As many ways as we can feel bad, weak, incompetent, unworthy and unloved, Satan will come up with a lie or deception to try to make us believe that. As he does so, we begin to embrace and treasure the lies until we reek of them. As a result, we become immobilized and ineffective.

How do we get the stench of those lies out of us? How do we get the scent of those lies out of the fabric of our being? By constantly flooding ourselves with the Truth. Christians are encouraged to feed each other truth so that the lies won't harm us. "Take care, brethren, that there not be in any one of you an evil, unbelieving heart that falls away from the living God. But encourage one another day after day, as long as it is still called 'Today,' so that none of you will be hardened by the deceitfulness of sin." Hebrews 3:12-13. Notice that it is possible for one of the "brethren" to have "an evil, unbelieving heart." It is our fellow Christian's job to help keep the "deceitfulness of sin" at bay.

There are times when dirt and smells are so imbedded into a fabric that once they are clean, there's a little something left behind. When we are washed in the pure blood of Christ, we are clean in His sight. But our belief systems do not immediately change. Reorienting our attitudes, takes a flooding of truth. Truth needs to wear away the stink of our false beliefs until the fresh Truth of God reshapes our beliefs and our personalities.

The *ekklesia* is made up of people who are overcoming false identities given to them by Satan. Although we are washed from our sins, the lies of our lifetimes may take years to overcome when we fail to acknowledge them. They cripple us. However, each member brings Christ's truths to the other members of the *ekklesia* so that every person can know the true image of himself or herself in Christ. We are not orphans. We have a Father who loves us and wants us to know our names. We have a family.

5: KNOWING WHO YOU ARE

If you ask members of the military who they are, they can tell you. They can tell you their rank, who their commanding officers are, who their subordinates are. They know their jobs. They know who their fellow soldiers are. They know who their allies are. Because they know where their allegiance lies, they also know who the enemy is. In short, it is critical for the members of the military to understand who they are. Without knowing their identity in the military, they are useless. To underscore the chaos and confusion during a battle scene in the movie *Apocalypse Now*, the main character asks a soldier he comes across in the trenches in a night battle, "Who's the commanding officer here?" The soldier answers, "Ain't you?" The soldiers were lost because they did not know who they were, who their leader was and who their enemy was.

Our identity. The fear of Yahveh is the beginning of knowledge. Proverbs 9:10. Knowing God also means to know that He has told us who we are. We are not left to try to understand ourselves on our own. We are not left to "feel" our way to self-knowledge: our hearts are deceptive. "The heart is more deceitful than all else and is desperately sick; Who can understand it? I, the Lord, search the heart, I test the mind, even to give to each man according to his ways, according to the results of his deeds." Jeremiah 17:9. God knows all of our thoughts, even our "secret" ones. Psalm 94:11 and 44:21. He knew us from before our bodies were formed: God knows us intimately. Psalm 139. Because of this, we are not left in an existential quagmire. God, who knows us better than we know ourselves, tells us who we are.

Christ's friends. God's friends. We were slaves of sin before we were redeemed. Romans 6. We were identified by the sins we had committed and the wrongs that were done. When we become Christians, we are defined by what God has made us to be. Jesus said, "Greater love has no one than this, that one lay down his life for his friends. You are My friends if you do what I command you. No longer do I call you slaves, for the slave does not know what his master is doing; but I have called you friends, for all things that I have heard from My Father I have made known to you." John 15. Jesus is speaking of us here, too, not just the twelve. He laid down His life for each and every Christian. This echoes what was said of Abraham in James 2: "You see that faith was working with his works, and as a result of the works, faith was perfected; and the Scripture was fulfilled which says, 'And Abraham believed God, and it was reckoned to him as righteousness,' and he was called the friend of God." As Christians, we are Abraham's descendants. Galatians 3:29. So we, like our father Abraham, have become friends of God and friends of His Son. God chooses who His friends are: not us.

God's children. His heirs. Before Christ's death, He said to the twelve, "I will not leave you as orphans." Christ has given us a family. We have a Father. We have Christ as our First-born Brother. We have brothers and sisters. Christ has given us an entire family. Christ is the firstborn of our big family. Romans 8:29. Christ, as our older brother is not ashamed to call us his "brothers." Hebrews 2:11. I am amazed that the Son of God considers us His siblings. Why are we his brothers and sisters? Because we have been selected to be adopted by God as His children. Romans 8 and Galatians 4. Not only do we have that vertical relationship with God as the Father who adopted us, we gain new horizontal relationships with our fellow adopted siblings! Jesus said, "Truly I say to you, there is no one who has left house or brothers or sisters or mother or father or children or farms, for My sake and for the gospel's sake, but that he will receive a hundred times as much now in the present age, houses and brothers and sisters and mothers and children and farms, along with persecutions; and in the age to come, eternal life." Mark 10:29-30.

Since we are God's children, we are God's heirs, co-inheritors with Christ. "The Spirit Himself testifies with our spirit that we are children of God, and if children, heirs also, heirs of God and fellow heirs with Christ, if indeed we suffer with Him so that we may also be glorified with Him." Romans 8:16-17. What are we heirs of? We inherit eternal life. Titus 3. We are heirs of the Kingdom of Heaven with Christ. James 2:5. As fellow-heirs of the Kingdom of Heaven, we will reign with Christ, and He will have us sit on His throne with Him. 2 Timothy 2:12 and Revelation 3:21.

Justified. As members of Christ's body, we are justified. What does it mean to be "justified"? *Justified* is a technical term meaning to declare or show to be free from blame or guilt; absolved. As Christians, we are free from blame or guilt. Have you committed heinous sins in the past? As a Christian, Christ has taken care of that punishment. We are free from all blame. Further more, we are free from all guilt. Sadly, many Churches use guilt to motivate their members. In Christ, there is no guilt. We have no reason to feel guilty about anything. Can we feel remorse or sadness? Yes. But not to the point where it wears us down and diminishes even a fraction of our justification before God.

Every Christian has heard "all have sinned and fallen short of the glory of God." Romans 3:23. Our shortcomings have been made up for through Christ. Christ Jesus is both "just and the justifier of the one who has faith" in Him. He is just as a judge, because a debt was owed and a punishment was due because of our sins. He is the justifier because He has paid the debt and taken on the punishment for sin. So that we can know that there is no condemnation for sin for those who are in Christ. Romans 8.

Glorified. Because we are justified, we are also glorified: "...these whom He justified, He also glorified." Romans 8:30. Through grace and through the blood of Christ, we have that glory – which we fell short of because of sin – restored. We have received the "glory of Christ." 2 Thessalonians 2:14 and 1 Peter 5:10. Now we are called "sons of glory:" the sons that Christ brought to glory through His sufferings. Hebrews 2:10.

One might say that we shouldn't seek glory for ourselves. We are not. We are seeking the glory that is given by God. Jesus criticized the Pharisees for not seeking that glory: "How can you believe, when you receive glory from one another and you do not seek the glory that is from the one and only God?" John 5:44. Paul talked of this in Romans 2 in comparing the stubbornly unrepentant with those who persevere, "seek for " and will ultimately receive glory:

> But because of your stubbornness and unrepentant heart you are storing up wrath for yourself in the day of wrath and revelation of the righteous judgment of God, who will render to each person according to his deeds: to those who by perseverance in doing good seek for glory and honor

and immortality, eternal life; but to those who are selfishly ambitious and do not obey the truth, but obey unrighteousness, wrath and indignation. There will be tribulation and distress for every soul of man who does evil...for there is no partiality with God.

From one point of view, the glorification of the children of God, Christians, is the purpose and climax of all creation. The revealing of the glory of the Children of God – the revealing of those who have been freed from slavery – is what all creation is yearning for: "For the anxious longing of the creation waits eagerly for the revealing of the sons of God. For the creation was subjected to futility, not willingly, but because of Him who subjected it, in hope that the creation itself also will be set free from its slavery to corruption into the freedom of the glory of the children of God." Romans 8:19-21.

How does this happen? It happens through the working of the Holy Spirit. In comparing how the glory of God shown through Moses's face, the ministry of the Holy Spirit comes with more glory: "For if that which fades away *was* with glory, much more that which remains *is* in glory." It is the Holy Spirit who is converting us into God's glory: "But we all, with unveiled face, beholding as in a mirror the glory of the Lord, are being transformed into the same image from glory to glory, just as from the Lord, the Spirit." 2 Corinthians 3. It is not uncommon for people to undergo plastic surgery to look like their favorite actor or actress. Here, however, the Holy Spirit is conducting plastic survey on our souls, making us into Christ's image.. As we are being transformed, we become unified with one another and with God and become that ultimate expression of God's love and God's glory: "The glory which You have given Me I have given to them, that they may be one, just as We are one; I in them and You in Me, that they may be perfected in unity, so that the world may know that You sent Me, and loved them, even as You have loved Me." John 17:22-23.

Blameless. Without spot or blemish. Accompanying the fact that we are glorified by Christ, is the fact that we are also holy and blameless. As Christians, we are part of that *ekklesia* that Christ "having cleansed her by the washing of water with the word, that He might present to Himself the *ekklesia* in all her glory, having no spot or wrinkle or any such thing; but that she would be holy and blameless." Ephesians 5: 27. As John said,

...but if we walk in the Light as He Himself is in the Light, we have fellowship with one another, and the blood of Jesus His Son cleanses us from all sin. If we say that we have no sin, we are deceiving ourselves and the truth is not in us. If we confess our sins, He is faithful and righteous to forgive us our sins and to cleanse us from all unrighteousness.

1 John 1:7-9. Here, too, the Holy Spirit is at work: "He saved us, not on the basis of deeds which we have done in righteousness, but according to His mercy, by the washing of regeneration and renewing by the Holy Spirit...." Titus 3:5. The word for regeneration in Greek means "born again" and echoes what Christ said in John 3: "Truly, truly, I say to you, unless one is born of water and the Spirit he cannot enter into the kingdom of God." We have both aspects of baptism: the washing with water and the spiritual rebirth. Then notice that the Holy Spirit is "renewing" us. *Strongs* defines this as "a renewal, renovation, complete change for the better." Each one of us is one of the Holy Spirit's renovation projects: He is continually renovating us.

Now, wait, this sounds too good to be true. However, it's exactly true: Christ made one sacrifice for all sins for all time. The Holy Spirit even testifies to the fullness of this forgiveness: "And their sins and their lawless deeds I will remember no more." Hebrews 10. How awesome is the very thought that with one sacrifice Our Lord has covered all our sins for all time. Does this mean that apostasy is impossible? No. "For if we go on sinning willfully after receiving the knowledge of the truth, there no longer remains a sacrifice for sins, but a terrifying expectation of judgment and the fury of a fire which will consume the adversaries." Hebrews 10. By our willful, continual sinning – a change away from our walk with God – we remove ourselves from that walk and from the benefits of the supreme sacrifice.

Filled up with love. Filled up with God. We know that God is love. We know that "the love of God has been poured out within our hearts through the Holy Spirit who was given to us." Romans 5. God does nothing half way. He fills us up to overflowing. Now, just how full are we filled with God? Just how full are we with Love? Paul explains this in Ephesians 3:14-21:

For this reason I bow my knees before the Father, from whom every family in heaven and on earth derives its name, that He would grant you, according to the riches of His glory, to be strengthened with power through His Spirit in the inner man, so that Christ may dwell in your hearts through faith; *and* that you, being rooted and grounded in love, may be able to comprehend with all the saints what is the breadth and length and height and depth, and to know the love of Christ which surpasses knowledge, that you may be filled up to all the fullness of God. Now to Him who is able to do far more abundantly beyond all that we ask or think, according to the power that works within us, to Him *be* the glory in the church and in Christ Jesus to all generations forever and ever. Amen.

First, Paul tells us that we "may be filled up to all the fullness of God." A friend who would often overeat would say, 'I'm full up to my lower lip." Being filled up to all the fullness, surpasses this. As David said, "My cup overflows," so our lives and our very beings can literally overflow with God. Paul's next sentence is just a hint at the extent that God can fill us to overflowing: "abundantly beyond all that we ask or think." In other words, we are filled up with God beyond our comprehension.

But wait: there's an apparent contradiction here! Paul says that we are "able to comprehend with all the saints what is the breadth and length and height and depth, and to know the love of Christ which surpasses knowledge." So Paul tells us we can comprehend the incomprehensible. We can know the unknowable. How? Paul tells us right up front: we are to be "strengthened with power through His Spirit in the inner man, so that Christ may dwell in your hearts through faith." In more detail, Paul explained it: "Now we have received, not the spirit of the world, but the Spirit who is from God, so that we may know the things freely given to us by God, which things we also speak, not in words taught by human wisdom, but in those taught by the Spirit, combining spiritual *thoughts* with spiritual *words*." 1 Corinthians 2:12-13 The power of the Helper allows us to comprehend. Without the Holy Spirit, we are unable to understand Christ. Without understanding Christ, we are unable to understand God and His love. The Holy Spirit, who dwells within each one of us, makes this otherwise incomprehensible knowledge comprehensible.

Loved. Peaceful. Ecstatic. Overjoyed. In Romans 5 Paul describes the wonderful relationship we now have with God:

Therefore, having been justified by faith, we have peace with God through our Lord Jesus Christ, through whom also we have obtained our introduction by faith into this grace in which we stand; and we exult in hope of the glory of God. And not only this, but we also exult in our tribulations, knowing that tribulation brings about perseverance; and perseverance, proven character; and proven character, hope; and hope does not disappoint, because the love of God has been poured out within our hearts through the Holy Spirit who was given to us. For while we were still helpless, at the right time Christ died for the ungodly. For one will hardly die for a righteous man; though perhaps for the good man someone would dare even to die. But God demonstrates His own love toward us, in that while we were yet sinners, Christ died for us. Much more then, having now been justified by His blood, we shall be saved from the wrath of God through Him. For if while we were enemies we were reconciled to God through the death of His Son, much more, having been reconciled, we shall be saved by His life. And not only this, but we also exult in God through our Lord Jesus Christ, through whom we have now received the reconciliation.

This description of us is awesome, breathtaking and humbling. What an amazing relationship we have with God! No other being has this relationship. Christ did not die for the angels. Satan and his demons have no hope for redemption. God made humans in such a way that He couldn't resist loving us. A friend described this beautifully: "The Maker of the universe would rather die for me than live without me!" Even though we alienated ourselves from God, He made a way so that we could have that relationship reestablished. From Romans 5 we know:

- We are at peace with God.
- We exult in the hope of the glory of God and in our tribulations. We also exult in God through Christ. *Exult* means to be "extremely joyful" and comes from the idea of "jumping for joy" and to be so extremely joyful we can hardly control ourselves.
- God poured love into our hearts to the point of overflowing.
- We have been justified. In God's eyes, we have no sin, and therefore, no punishment for sin. "...we shall be saved from the wrath of God..."
- We have been reconciled. Once we were enemies. Now we are His children and His friends. Our sins once separated us from God. Christ has taken away the enmity that we once had.

The Holy Spirit has been given to us. No other people have had this blessing. The Holy Spirit was not given to all of Israel: He was given to us! He, too, has been poured into our hearts and has taken up residence.

Royalty. Priests of the Most High God. Peter tell us that we are "a chosen race, a royal priesthood, a holy nation, a people for God's own possession." 1 Peter 2. We are adopted children of God. Romans 8 and Galatians 4. Because Christ is the King, then we, as his brothers and sisters, are princes and princesses. God has made us into a Kingdom of Priests. Revelation 1:6, 5:10 and 20:6. When we overcome this world, He will give us power and will bring us up to sit with Him on His throne. Revelation 2:26 and 3:21. As Christians, God has made us royalty in the highest kingdom that has ever existed. We are a pure, holy priesthood. When you look at fellow Christians, do you see a holy, royal nation of priests? When you look in the mirror, do you see royalty? God sees you that way.

Who are you? Who does God say you are? The only truly objective being in the universe is God. Reality and Truth can only be defined by God, because He is the only being who can view His Creation from the outside. Understanding God's view of us should give us great comfort. We are not who we are because of our own doing. We are who we are through the selfless sacrifice of a God overflowing with love.

If someone were to ask you who you are, do you have an answer now? If you were asked to describe yourself, how would you do so? If we see ourselves in any way other than the way God has made us to be, we are listening to lies from Satan from the very pit of hell. However, if someone were to draw a portrait of you as God sees you, the portrait would be indescribably beautiful. God's *ekklesia* is filled with just such people.

Too often Churches emphasize our guilt, sinfulness, worthlessness, or some other distorted picture. Unwittingly, people cling to that distorted view and feel the need for the Church to plaster over their imperfections or to give them morphine to dull the pain of the lies about their false identity. The *ekklesia* does not. The *ekklesia* is filled with glorified, beautiful, happy, pure, God-filled, royal priests, who are God's children and God's friends. Each person in the *ekklesia* sees other Christians and themselves in the same way.

The identity of the individuals belonging to a group defines, in part, the group itself. As individuals we are friends of God and Christ. God has adopted us as His children and made us heirs to all that he possesses. God, through Christ has also made up for all of our shortcomings, justifying us in God's sight so we are blameless and spotless. We are glorified and filled up with God Himself. We are royal priests, full of love, peace, joy and compassion. We are ecstatic and overjoyed. Now imagine a group of people just like you are in the same place at the same time. As Christians join together, these attributes multiply. Pure, holy, blameless, rejoicing ecstatically. Royal children of God ministering to one another in sacrificial love.

6: SPIRITUAL HOBOS

During the mid-nineteenth century and until about 1939, a unique subculture developed in the United States. It consisted mostly of penniless, homeless men. Popularly they were thought of as criminals and were pursued viciously by law enforcement; but, for the most part they were far from felons. Sometimes they were lumped together with tramps who worked only when they had to or bums who avoided work altogether. They were abused, beaten and shunned by much of society. They were hobos. H. L. Menken described these individuals as "simply a migratory laborer; he may take some longish holidays, but soon or late he returns to work."[16] Tramps wanted handouts; hobos wanted work.[17] Though separate wanderers, they shared a common identity and ethic. They came from all strata of life: some were intelligent and became attorneys, elected officials and writers, such as Ernest Hemingway and Jack London. Others became famous actors, such as Clark Gable. They formed their own Hobo Code of Conduct. Even though these men were separate wanderers, they formed a camaraderie as they hitched rides on railroad cars back and forth across the country. They even referred to themselves as a "brotherhood."[18] There is even a National Hobo Convention, which continues to this day in Britt, Iowa.[19] Though penniless and homeless, these hobos had treasures. Their treasures are similar to the treasures that Christians have, too.

The hobos were not unlike those described in Hebrews 11 who wandered the earth:

---

[16] H. L. Mencken, *The American Language*, 581.

[17] "Steam Train" Maury Graham and Hemming, Robert J., *Tales of the Iron Road,*" 62.

[18] Ted Connover, *Rolling Nowhere*, 93.

[19] http://www.hobo.com/convention.html, retrieved April 8, 2013.

All these ... having confessed that they were strangers and exiles on the earth. For those who say such things make it clear that they are seeking a country of their own. And indeed if they had been thinking of that country from which they went out, they would have had opportunity to return. But as it is, they desire a better country, that is, a heavenly one ... others experienced mocking and scourging, yes, also chains and imprisonment. They were stoned, they were sawn in two, they were tempted, they were put to death with the sword; they went about in sheepskins, in goatskins, being destitute, afflicted, ill-treated (*men* of whom the world was not worthy), wandering in deserts and mountains and caves and holes in the ground.

Hebrews 11:13-16 and 36-38. Although they came from different places, cultures and times, all these people had a common goal and identity: they were all sojourning aliens. Abraham first sojourned in the land of promise. Hebrews 11:9. We Christians are described as aliens here on this earth. 1 Peter 1:1 and 2:11. The fact that we Christians have a new citizenship necessarily makes us aliens here. "So then you are no longer strangers and aliens, but you are fellow citizens with the saints, and are of God's household..." Ephesians 2:19. Contrary to what many people want, dual citizenship is not an option.

Now as aliens living in an foreign country or world, this *should* establish a new set of values for us. It means that what we have here is ephemeral. Abraham lived in tents: temporary structures meant to be moved about. The tents were physical testimonies to his "alienness." The nation of Israel celebrated the "Feast of Booths" – which was a time when all Israel went outside their houses and lived in tents: they camped in their backyards to remember how their ancestors lived. Transiently. Temporarily. Just passing through. Living like hobos. As the modern spiritual Israel, we are just passing though this world. Therefore, a whole new set of values springs up for us. It is really sad that we don't know or see true hobos today – persons for whom possessions have no value and who are "homeless" without needing a home. They were not lazy; they were just people for whom physical possessions meant nothing. They were destitute, afflicted, ill-treated, wandering in deserts and mountains and caves and holes in the ground. Should we Christians should emulate these hobos?

Proper valuation. As Peter said, "Since all these things are to be destroyed in this way, what sort of people ought you to be in holy conduct and godliness, looking for and hastening the coming of the day of God, because of which the heavens will be destroyed by burning, and the elements will melt with intense heat!" 2 Peter 3:11-12. If a building were temporary or were to be destroyed, what attachment would you have for it? During the Falles Festival in Valencia, Spain, communities build elaborate, giant statues of paper, cork and wood. The statues represent things they consider repressive in their lives. At the end of the festival, all the statues are burned. The burning of the statues symbolizes liberation from the things the statues represent. We likewise are living in a world destined to be incinerated – and all of these earthly things can repress us in one way or another. So how tightly should we clench onto the ephemeral, soon-to-be-burned "treasures" of this world?

Jesus said it straightforward and clearly: "Do not store up for yourselves treasures on earth, where moth and rust destroy, and where thieves break in and steal. But store up for yourselves treasures in heaven, where neither moth nor rust destroys, and where thieves do not break in or steal; for where your treasure is, there your heart will be also." Matthew 6:19-21. Jesus lovingly teases us into thought. Truly great teachers do not give you the answers: they teach you how to find the answers on your own. Jesus, the greatest teacher, told us directly what the treasure *isn't*. Our treasures are not things of this world.

Collecting treasure. Jesus also let us know the treasures we lay up in heaven are not our good works in this life. A compliment I have heard often is "She'll get a special star in her crown in heaven." That is nowhere in the scriptures. Whatever we do in this life to serve God, is exactly what we *should* be doing anyway. Meditate on this: what is there that we can give the God of the universe, the Creator of all that exists, that can have value to Him? Jesus told a parable, in which after the servants had completed everything they were required to do, they said, "We are unworthy slaves; we have done only that which we ought to have done." Luke 17:10.[20] Our works do nothing for us. If we obey the law, what is that to God? So what can we offer God? What if we were to speak with the tongues of men and of angels;

---

[20] In reality, this is a beautiful parable about grace.

have the gift of prophecy; know all mysteries; have all knowledge; have all faith, so as to remove mountains; and give all our possessions to feed the poor, and surrender our bodies to be burned, would that be anything less that what would be expected of us as faithful servants? See 1 Corinthians 13.

Nevertheless, Christ told us to pursue this treasure with everything we have. In two parables, He told us of a man who sold everything so he could possess the "treasure hidden in a field," and the "pearl of great value." Matthew 13.

Weeding. Jesus told us what gets in our way of receiving this treasure that we can lay up in heaven in the parable of the sower. Remember that seed, the word of God, fell upon different types of soil. Some seed fell on ground where there were thorns: "And the one on whom seed was sown among the thorns, this is the man who hears the word, and the worry of the world and the deceitfulness of wealth choke the word, and it becomes unfruitful." Other seed fell on good soil, that is good hearts: "And the one on whom seed was sown on the good soil, this is the man who hears the word and understands it; who indeed bears fruit and brings forth, some a hundredfold, some sixty, and some thirty." Matthew 13:22-23. So what might get in the way of our being fruitful and laying up treasures? Worldly worries and worldly wealth. Notice if you will what Jesus characterizes as "good soil": it is soil that has neither the care of the world or the treasures or wealth of this world. In other words, the good soil is poor people. "...Did not God choose the poor of this world to be rich in faith and heirs of the kingdom which He promised to those who love Him?" James 2:5. The poor are those "patches of soil" that are free of weeds.

With all this in mind, the intimate conversation that Jesus had with the rich young man reverberates with a much deeper meaning. In Mark 10:17-22, a rich young ruler asked the Master of the Universe what he needed to do to inherit eternal life. Jesus felt love for him. Christ's special compassion for an individual shows nothing less than the sincerity, and genuineness of that man's heart. So Jesus said, "One thing you lack: go and sell all you possess and give to the poor, and you will have treasure in heaven; and come, follow Me." It was not the act of giving to the poor that would make this rich, young ruler a follower: it was the weeding of his garden – so to speak.

When Christ calls His first followers, Peter, Andrew, James and John, they weeded themselves. Peter and Andrew "immediately they left their nets and followed Him." James and John "immediately they left the boat and their father, and followed Him." Matthew 4. Mark 1.

Even with Jesus we see Him "weeding" Himself. He had already placed Himself in poor circumstances: He "emptied Himself, taking the form of a bond-servant." Philippians 2. But, He also divested Himself of His earthly family. When His mother and brothers came looking for Him in Mark 3:33-35, Jesus said, "'Who are My mother and My brothers?' Looking about at those who were sitting around Him, He said, 'Behold My mother and My brothers! For whoever does the will of God, he is My brother and sister and mother.'" Why were they looking for Jesus? Our best answer would only be a guess. The bigger question would be, where was Joseph? It would appear that at this time Joseph was either ill or dead. Joseph and Mary together searched for Him when Jesus was 12 and "lost." Luke 2. With Joseph absent, Jesus would have been the new "head" of his family. The position of the oldest son in middle-eastern society is critical: even today, a widow without a son as the "head of the household" may starve. Jesus gave up these worldly-weedy entanglements to his younger brothers at that time. However, this did not meant that Jesus abandoned Mary: even as He was dying, Jesus gave the care of Mary to John. John 19.

Fireproof treasures. There is an old Jack Benny joke. Benny was a comedian from the days of Vaudeville and later radio. A running gag with Benny was how tightly he held onto his money. In one comedy bit, the straight-man told Benny, "You can't take your money with you when you die." Benny's response was, "I don't know about that. I've got an asbestos suitcase." But, in a strange sense, Jack Benny was right.

Paul told the Christians in Corinth how to put their treasures in "asbestos suitcases" in a manner of speaking. In 1 Corinthians 3, Paul said,

> According to the grace of God which was given to me, like a wise master builder I laid a foundation, and another is building on it. But each man must be careful how he builds on it. For no man can lay a foundation other than the one which is laid, which is Jesus Christ. Now if any man builds on the foundation with gold, silver, precious stones, wood, hay, straw, each man's work will become evident; for the day will show it

because it is *to be* revealed with fire, and the fire itself will test the quality of each man's work. If any man's work which he has built on it remains, he will receive a reward. If any man's work is burned up, he will suffer loss; but he himself will be saved, yet so as through fire.

What was this thing Paul was building? The metaphor is there that tells us: Jesus Christ is the foundation stone and Paul is the master builder.[21] Paul makes it clear in Ephesians 2:

So then you are no longer strangers and aliens, but you are fellow citizens with the saints, and are of God's household, having been built on the foundation of the apostles and prophets, Christ Jesus Himself being the corner *stone*, in whom the whole building, being fitted together, is growing into a holy temple in the Lord, in whom you also are being built together into a dwelling of God in the Spirit.

Peter even explains it further in 1 Peter 2:

And coming to Him as to a living stone which has been rejected by men, but is choice and precious in the sight of God, you also, as living stones, are being built up as a spiritual house for a holy priesthood, to offer up spiritual sacrifices acceptable to God through Jesus Christ. For *this* is contained in Scripture: "Behold, I lay in Zion a choice stone, a precious corner*stone*, And he who believes in Him will not be disappointed." This precious value, then, is for you who believe;... But you are a chosen race, a royal priesthood, a holy nation, a people for *God's* own possession, so that you may proclaim the excellencies of Him who has called you out of darkness into His marvelous light; for you once were not a people, but now you are the people of God; you had not received mercy, but now you have received mercy.

What is this thing that we are builders of? We are builders of the *ekklesia*. This spiritual building, this *ekklesia,* is all made up of relationships. Peter describes us is a series of relationships. See how we are described:

- *fellow citizens with the saints*: we have a relationship with each other having a common citizenship.
- *a spiritual house*: we are interrelated components of the same building.

---

[21] A master builder was a man who acted as an architect, engineer and construction foreman.

- *a holy, royal priesthood*: a priest has a special relationship with God; and as a priest*hood* we share together in our duties.
- *a chosen race*: we are all come from the same spiritual, genetic material because we have the same Father and were made from Christ, out of the side of the Spiritual Adam.
- *a holy nation and a people for God's own possession*: as fellow citizens possessed by God, we all have a common bond between us, not to mention our relationship with God!.
- *recipients of mercy*: this demonstrates our relationship with God

The *ekklesia* is not an organization or an institution. The *ekklesia* is described as the nation, the priesthood, the building, the family: these are all physical descriptions of spiritual *relationships*! Christ did not die so we could have a religious institution or organization; Christ died so we could have a relationship with God!

Look back at the works of men that endure through fire described in 1 Corinthians 3. What is it that we can send ahead of us to Heaven or that we can store "up there?" It is relationships. James said that if we help rescue a brother who has turned aside, that we "cover a multitude of sins." James 5. Peter said it a different way: "Above all, keep fervent in your love for one another, because love covers a multitude of sins." 1 Peter 4. It's about creating relationships and reestablishing a straying Christian's relationship with God. The relationships are our treasure. We have a stronger bond with God and, therefore, a stronger bond with our brothers and sisters. The gold, silver and precious stones that survive the test of fire can't be works. Doing good and sacrificing is just what Christians do: feeding the poor, caring for the sick, caring for those in prisons, lifting up the downcast. You don't get rewarded for doing your duty. Unless we turn a heart to God or help a fellow Christian toward a closer relationship with God, we are doing good earthly works which do not endure, even though *we* will be saved.

What was the rock, the cornerstone and foundation, upon which Jesus was going to build His *ekklesia*? It is the fact that Jesus has a relationship with God. It is also the fact that Christ promised that we could have a relationship with Him. That foundation was this fact: "You are the Christ, the Son of the living God." Matthew 16:16. The "son" relationship shows His connection with God. The "Christ" relationship shows His relationship with us.

Remember the hobos? They had treasures. Physical possessions and earthly connections tied them down: these things burdened and choked out their nature as wanderers. "Let the nomads of the desert bow before him..." Psalm 72. Because they had no homes, no money, and no family, their relationships with each other became their only treasures. As earthly hobos, we have a much richer treasure: not just a relationship with each other but also a relationship with God. That is why God chose the poor of this world to be rich in faith and heirs of the kingdom which He promised to those who love Him. James 2:5.

The *ekklesia* is made up of relationships. As sojourners in this world, we put no value on possessions, positions or pride. We are laying up for ourselves valuable relationships: a relationship with God, first, and then relationships with our fellow sojourners. Those are treasures that will not rust and no moth can touch. No man can steal them. They are treasures that will endure the fire and last forever.

PART THREE: BELONGING

TOM MANN

7: HEARING THE TOWN CRYER

On the first Monday in October, the Marshall of the Supreme Court of the United States of America shouts in the courtroom, "Oyez! Oyez! Oyez! All persons having business before the Honorable, the Supreme Court of the United States, are admonished to draw near and give their attention, for the Court is now sitting. God save the United States and this Honorable Court." This formal pronouncement has begun sessions of the court for centuries. Its roots are deeper than that. "Oyez" was a term used by town criers to get the attention of people and to gather a crowd or a select group of people. The voices of town criers are silent today. They've been silenced by newspaper, radio, television, the internet, and text messaging. Today, electronic media have created a new version of that gathering: the flashmob.

A flashmob is brought together by a message being sent out, either through texts, Twitter or FaceBook. They come together for a specific purpose. Sometimes they assemble for a protest. Other times they assemble to do something amazing. One emotionally moving flashmob was an "impromptu" singing of Handel's Hallelujah Chorus in a food court in a shopping mall in Ohio in 2010.[22] It starts with a single woman's voice. A man joins in. By the end, the concrete mall echoes with praise that no one can ignore or denigrate. The video on YouTube brings many people to tears. The unity of its voice, its common message, and the volume of its Good News are overwhelming without being wielded by a sledgehammer. Some were moved to tears. No person alive can deny its power. Hold this thought for just a moment: a modern town crier assembling a special group of people for an outpouring of praise to God that at the same time serenades the Gospel of Christ to everyone nearby. This sounds similar to Pliny the

---

[22] http://www.youtube.com/watch?v=SXh7JR9oKVE, retrieved October 31, 2013.

Younger's description of Christians meeting early in the morning singing responsive praises. The idea of the *ekklesia* is very similar.

First, the term *ekklesia* comes from Greek: *kaleo* "to call" and *ek* "out from." In ancient Athens the *ekklesia* was the popular assembly of the city to conduct city business and was open to all male citizens who had done military service, regardless of class. In Athens it sometimes met as often as four times a month. "In classical Greek, *ekklesia* referred to an assembly of citizens summoned by the town crier. It is used in Acts 19:32-41 in its purely classical meaning. The town clerk dismissed the citizens who had been gathered together by the craftsmen of Ephesus...."[23]

In our modern times, an *ekklesia* is probably the most similar to a New England town hall meeting. Town hall meetings are gatherings in which the members of the community voice opinions and ask questions of the public officials. Historically, there were no specific rules or guidelines for holding a town hall meeting. The concerns of individual citizens formed the agenda. When I mentioned this concept to a friend of mine from New Hampshire, she was a little confused. She said, "Have you ever been to a town hall meeting? They can get quite rowdy!" But then, I have read 1 Corinthians and realize that an *ekklesia* can get rowdy, too, even though it should not be. Otherwise, Paul wouldn't have had to say, "But all things must be done properly and in an orderly manner." 1 Corinthians 14:40. Remember also, that the town clerk in Ephesus quieted the assembly so certain persons could be heard, and the matter could be referred to and settled the legal tribunals: the proper venue for the silversmiths' complaints. Acts 19:39. There was not complete disorder. So the pastors of the *ekklesia* should preserve the order.

For a long time I was told that the crowd in Ephesus, an *ekklesia*, was a riotous, out of control mob – far from the idea I had of an *ekklessia*. I believed that until I had a non-religious *"ekklesia"* experience. I live in the Tampa area. In 2003, the Tampa Bay Buccaneers won the Super Bowl. As part of the victory celebration, the team opened the home stadium and gave everyone free entrance to welcome the team back. There were no tickets, no assigned seats and no special planned program. The stadium became packed almost to capacity while the jumbo television showed the team's plane landing at the airport nearby. Fans cheerfully talked to other fans. As tens of

---

[23] Kenneth S. Wuest, *Studies in the Vocabulary of the Greek New Testament*, 27.

thousands watched the buses arrive, cheers broke out in sections. When the players arrived on the field, spontaneous but coordinated cheers broke out everywhere. One side of the field shouted, "Tampa" and the other side answered, "Bay." The Coach and a local celebrity quieted the crowd. There were a few short speeches. The Lombardi trophy was flashed around. The team left the field, and the tens of thousands of people joyously left having experienced a celebratory unity. The experience was thrilling, exciting and unifying. The experience was an *ekklesia*.

Think about what an "assembly" of people can be. In high school we had pep rallies. We have assemblies of political parties called conventions. Legislatures assemble so that each representative and senator can participate. If a legislator (or *assemblyman* as they used to be called) never spoke or voted, he would not be doing his job. The very action of calling people to be assembled brings an expectation of action and activity. Activities are about to occur. Not only that, but whatever is going to occur will involve those people who assembled. Those assembled cannot be passive witnesses.

But I rarely think of people sitting quietly in rows facing forward in a dark movie theater to be an assembly. The original idea of an *ekklesia* was not a passive observation of a show or a performance. The Greek idea of an *ekklesia* always involved people assembling to share and to participate!

So when someone in the first century heard the term *ekklesia*, what image did it conjure? They thought of a special group of people brought together by a town crier. They thought of a group of people from all classes of society mingled together in one group. They thought of unorchestrated meetings where no one sat passively. They knew that each member of the *ekklesia* was free to participate and were usually expected to participate. The leading members of the *ekklesia* had an essential role in keeping the meeting or discussion orderly. The leaders did not necessarily do the majority of the speaking

How close is that to your idea of Church? In the chapters ahead, let's examine the scriptures to reassemble what God's *ekklesia* really is.

The *ekklesia* was originally a group of people from all classes of society coming together in a common meeting. An *ekklesia* was a gathering in which all members participated in an orderly way.

8: AUDIENCE OR PARTICIPANT?

Everyone has watched a comedy on television or watched a comic perform on stage. Everyone is in a group laughing and enjoying the performance. They are part of an audience. Have you ever been to an improvisational theater where members of the audience are called onto the stage and become part of the show? The improv actors call members out of the audience, gather them up on the stage and the audience members become part of the performance. They are gathered up on the stage for a purpose: they become participants.

Two words. Two roles. There are two words used in the Book of Exodus that are both translated either "congregation" or "assembly." Both words refer to a group of people, but the two groups are very different. As the "sons of Israel" become the "nation of Israel," God chooses different words used to describe them and their function. The first, `edah, refers to people gathered to witness, hear or experience an event: an audience. It comes from the word meaning "witness." The second word, qahal, means a gathering for a purpose, a group of people acting together as a community. The nation of Israel started out as an unorganized group of people who were spoken to. They were gathered for information to be given to them. Through a number of events the group changes. Israel becomes a collective group acting together.

The purpose for Moses to gather the sons of Israel was to tell them something. In each incident, the people are gathered as an audience: the "congregation of Israel." The word God used was `edah, which means a congregation or gathering, but it comes from a root word meaning *witness*. So this congregation was a passive one receiving instructions. Probably a more modern term would be *audience*. But, they were still just a passive group receiving information. God continues to refer to them as a passive group brought together to hear and witness the message Moses and Aaron delivered.

Next, something wonderful happens. When the Israelites were in Egypt, they were slaves of the Egyptians. They did not function as a nation or a community: Pharaoh said only that they "filled our country." The Egyptians were afraid that they might *become* a singular group, join with a foreign nation and take over Egypt. Exodus 1:9-10. As Moses passed on God's demands to Pharaoh and as the plagues tortured the Egyptians, a little glimmer that the sons of Israel would come together and act as an assembled community. Not an audience. Just before the last plague, just before the first Passover, the audience starts to become a participating body:

Your lamb shall be an unblemished male a year old; you may take it from the sheep or from the goats. You shall keep it until the fourteenth day of the same month, then the whole assembly [participating] of the congregation [audience] of Israel is to kill it at twilight. Exodus 12:5-7. By participating together in the first Passover, they start to function together, or at least start to change from a passive audience of people to an assembled, active community. The story doesn't end there; it is just beginning.

Now here is where it gets fun. After God delivers them and brings the people to Mount Sinai, He also changes the word He uses to describe the "congregation of the Sons of Israel." The word to describe Israel reappears: *qahal,* which is virtually the same as both a noun and a verb, meaning to assemble or gather or an assembly or gathering. The people consecrated themselves for two days, washing their garments. On the third day they were to approach, but not go on, the mountain. On that third day God spoke to Israel from the mountain, giving them the Ten Commandments. They were gathered together as a *qahal*, they pleaded with Moses not to have God speak to them directly any longer. God recognized their unity in action when He said, "<u>They</u> have spoken well." Deuteronomy 5:22 and 18:16-17.

If you've stuck with me this long and haven't nodded off a couple of times while reading this, you may think this is a lot of quibbling over small words and names. However, I hope you change your mind, because it was at this precise point in the history of Israel that God first called any group an *ekklesia.*

The first *ekklesia*. When Stephen was giving his defense, he recounted the history of the nation of Israel. Stephen called those people, a nation called out of Egypt, baptized in the sea, under a special covenant with God, gathered in the wilderness and acting together with a purpose: an *ekklesia*! "This is the one who was in the congregation (*ekklesia*) in the wilderness together with the angel who was speaking to him on Mount Sinai, and who was with our fathers; and he received living oracles to pass on to you." Acts 7:38.

The idea of a group of people being gathered together with a purpose to act was not always pretty. When Korah led the rebellion in the desert, the people "gathered" against Moses and Aaron. Numbers 16. Several times the "congregation" "gathered" itself to rebel. The body of people became gathered for a purpose. Joshua 18:1, 22:12. A remarkable example of this is metaphorically described in Judges 20:1: the "congregation" "assembled" "as one man."

The *ekklesia* in prophecy. God starts using the word *qahal*, an active assembly prophetically through Isaac. Picture the scene: Jacob has just swindled his brother Esau out of his inheritance and his blessing. Jacob is running away because he is afraid Esau will kill him. Jacob's father says to him: "May God Almighty bless you and make you fruitful and multiply you, that you may become a company of peoples. Genesis 28:3. But the phrase *"company of peoples"* is better translated "an assembly of peoples." (See *Young's Literal Translation*.) When God renamed Jacob Israel, He also told him, "A nation and a company of nations shall come from you, And kings shall come forth from you." Again "a company of nations" is better translated "an assembly of nations." (See Young's Literal Translation.) Or, both of these phrases might be better described as "an actively united gathering of people." In a single word, it is a Community.[24] The word used both times is *qahal*. God is talking about an *ekklesia* of people, an *ekklesia* of nations.

How does this story of Israel becoming a nation help us understand what an *ekklesia* is? First, the way Stephen uses the word lets us know the *ekklesia* is a *qahal*: it is not passive a audience. When people were gathered to have information given to them, they were passive. They were an audience. They were not a *qahal*. Second, it demonstrates the nature of the type of gathering. It is not just people being herded together: it is a

---

[24] One organization defined a "community of nations" as "An idea advocating peace and mediation, rather than policies of militarism and imperialism, and based on the interests of all nations." That sounds more like how Communities (Churches) should act rather than vicious debates and squabbles and divisions that often erupt.

group of people with much in common: a common history, fellowship and destination. Third, it shows that they were collectively active as a community. It's our first picture of the *ekklesia*.

God painted a picture of what an *ekklesia* is: it is an active community of people, all working together with a common heritage, a common salvation, and a common destination. It is not a passive audience. In an *ekklesia*, all members participate.

PART FOUR: REASSEMBLING THE PIECES

TOM MANN

9: LITTLE MODELS

What Americans call the *Statute of Liberty* isn't its real name. Frédéric Bartholdi titled his work *Liberty Enlightening the World.* (Actually, *La Liberté éclairant le monde,* because he was French.) Americans know the French gave them the 151 foot tall statue gracing New York harbor which was dedicated on October 28, 1886. But the American's *Statute of Liberty* is not the original. In reality, *La Liberté éclairant le monde* began as a flat drawing. The flat drawing was made into several smaller three dimensional models: the American statue is a final realization of the smaller ones. Parts of the statue were assembled and displayed around the world so people could have an idea of what the enormous scale of this statue would be. The right arm and torch were exhibited in New York at the 1876 Centennial Exhibition. The statue's head was exhibited at the Paris World's Fair in 1878. Smaller complete models were circulated so people could have an idea of what the final work would look like.

In a similar way, God has given us physical models to demonstrate ultimate spiritual realities. As Bartholdi's flat drawing, turned into a clay model, then into a bronze model, then into his ultimate realization that we view in New York harbor; God has revealed His sketches, models, and drawings of His *ekklesia* throughout the Law, the Prophets and the Psalms. As we examine Bartholdi's drawings and models, we gain a better understanding of his final masterpiece. As we examine God's previews, we gain a deeper understanding into the masterpiece of His creation, His *ekklesia*, the Bride of Christ, the New Jerusalem.

A commonwealth. Several of the older states in the United States don't call themselves states: Kentucky, Massachusetts, Pennsylvania and Virginia call themselves commonwealths. The Oxford English Dictionary defines a commonwealth as "The whole body of people constituting a nation or state, the body politic; the state, an independent community, especially viewed as a body in which the whole people have a voice or interest." When Israel took possession, they had no earthly king. They had Yahveh as their King. They were separate tribes, or communities, of one nation all coexisting as one people. They were a commonwealth.

Individual tribes were governed by the elders of individual cities and tribes. When Israel sinned and forsook God, neighboring nations attacked or oppressed them. God would raise up a judge to activate the nation to deliver them from their oppressors. This lasted until they forgot God and started sinning again. It was a repetitive cycle. Judges 2:11-23.

This picture of Israel acting as a *qahal*, appears in the Book of Judges. When the men of Gibeah, of the tribe of Benjamin, raped and murdered a Levite's concubine, the unnamed Levite rallied the *qahal* so they acted together as one. "The chiefs of all the people, *even* of all the tribes of Israel, took their stand in the assembly [*qahal*] of the people of God, 400,000 foot soldiers who drew the sword...Then all the people arose as one man...." Judges 20.

An army. We also have a picture of what God had in mind for his "assembly." David gives us a picture of what this assembly – this *qahal* – is today. King Saul's army was caught in a stalemate. The Philistine's champion, Goliath, terrorized and taunted the army daily. David, a handsome youth of short stature, showed up and courageously challenged the giant. Goliath was offended that a runt of a boy came to fight him. "Am I a dog, that you come to me with sticks?" David set him straight:

> You come to me with a sword, a spear, and a javelin, but I come to you in the name of the Lord of hosts, the God of the armies of Israel, whom you have taunted. This day the Lord will deliver you up into my hands, and I will strike you down and remove your head from you. And I will give the dead bodies of the army of the Philistines this day to the birds of the sky and the wild beasts of the earth, that all the earth may know that there is a God in Israel, and that all this assembly [*qahal*] may know that the Lord does not deliver by sword or by spear; for the battle is the Lord's and He will give you into our hands.

1 Samuel 17. This army, dressed for battle, that in just minutes after this speech, would defeat the Philistine army was a *qahal*. So we have a picture of the *qahal* or *ekklesia* as a coordinated, assembly of soldiers: an army armed and ready-for-battle.

Temple builders. Worshippers. There is a beautiful picture of Israel at the height of the kingdom when it was united. David was nearing the end of his life, and God chose Solomon to be the next king. David speaks to the assembly [*qahal*] and challenges them with the task of building the Temple. The leaders offered willingly and together committed to the building Everyone rejoiced together because they were united in the task. together. Then in the presence of this unified group – this *qahal* or *ekklesia* – David praised God. "So David blessed the Lord in the sight of all the assembly [*qahal*]...." Then after accepting this mighty task, the assembly [*qahal*] worshipped God and celebrated:

> Then David said to all the assembly [*qahal*], "Now bless the Lord your God." And all the assembly [*qahal*] blessed the Lord, the God of their fathers, and bowed low and did homage to the Lord and to the king. On the next day they made sacrifices to the Lord and offered burnt offerings to the Lord, 1,000 bulls, 1,000 rams *and* 1,000 lambs, with their drink offerings and sacrifices in abundance for all Israel. So they ate and drank that day before the Lord with great gladness.

1 Chronicles 29. They were a united, participating assembly. This is not unique to this situation. In 2 Chronicles 29-30 we see the assembly [*qahal*] of Israel committing to worshipping God. Under Hezekiah, they offered sacrifices, thank offerings, observed the Passover, and the Feast of Unleavened Bread. Under Nehemiah, the assembly [*qahal*] began observing the Feast of the Tabernacles again. Nehemiah 8. These were individual acts of worship, but were done as part of that assembly, company, and community. These are individual acts done as a *qahal. A*s an *ekklesia*. As one man.

Learning and growing together. In Nehemiah, God reveals the unity of the *qahal*. The people were gathered "as one man" and are described as a *qahal*, an assembly. So what did this group of people acting as one man do? Nehemiah describes it:

> Then Ezra the priest brought the law before the assembly [*qahal*] of men, women and all who could listen with understanding, on the first day of the seventh month. He read from it before the square which was in front of the Water Gate from early morning until midday, in the presence of men and women, those who could understand; and all the people were attentive to the book of the law... Ezra opened the book in the sight

of all the people for he was standing above all the people; and when he opened it, all the people stood up. Then Ezra blessed the Lord the great God. And all the people answered, "Amen, Amen!" while lifting up their hands; then they bowed low and worshiped the Lord with their faces to the ground. Also ... the Levites, explained the law to the people while the people remained in their place. They read from the book, from the law of God, translating to give the sense so that they understood the reading.

Nehemiah 8. This was not a passive group of people. They were actively participating in learning the Law of Moses. They praised God. They all participated in the teaching, learning and praising. They asked questions while assembled. They were a community of learners. They were a *qahal*. They were an *ekklesia*.

Models of the *ekklesia*. From Stephen, we know that the *qahal* or *ekklesia* was in the wilderness. As we observe the history of Israel unfolding, we see how it functioned as a community. It was not a passive audience, even when they were being taught. Israel was a unified body, acting "as one man." This is a picture of the *ekklesia* as one body, acting together as one person. The *ekklesia* is one body. 1 Corinthians 12. Similar to the functioning of an army or group, each member of the body is essential to its function. Ephesians 4. We are also those who are being built into a Holy Temple. Ephesians 2. Through the pattern of the *qahal* of Israel, we are to teach each other that we all are being built into a Community of believers. Romans 15:14 and Colossians 3:16.

As Bartholdi's models and previews gave the world an idea of what his final masterpiece would look like, God's models of the *ekklesia* reveal to us details of what was in the mind of God. The *ekklesia* is unified, functioning "as one man": it is one body. The *ekklesia* is an equipped, coordinated army actively engaged in spiritual warfare. The *ekklesia* is a group of builders, building up a Holy Temple for God. We are both the builders and the building. The *ekklesia* is a group individuals involved in common worship and praise. The *ekklesia* is actively teaching itself and growing. God's *ekklesia* is a united, unstoppable body, coordinated in fulfilling God's mission using the involvement of every individual member. Rather than people sitting in pews being told what to do, what to sing and what to think, the *ekklesia* is a dynamic living body fueled by an unquenchable thirst for righteousness and powered by the Holy Spirit Himself.

The *ekklesia* is a community of people that look out for each other's welfare. The *ekklesia* is a community of builders engaged in building up a spiritual Temple for God. The *ekklesia* is an army equipped to fight spiritual battles, so connected that the members act "as one man." It is also a group of people that actively teaches each other, learns from each other, and edifies each other. And all the while, it is a community the worships and praises God.

10: CHIPPING AWAY AT THE BLOCK

When I was a kid in the 1960s, elephant jokes were very popular. I remember having a little book of elephant jokes, and I memorized many of them to impress my friends. They were usually silly and, therefore, very popular among children. They always had the same form, a question followed by an answer. One was, "Question: How do you carve a statue of an elephant? Answer: You get a big block of stone and take away everything that doesn't look like an elephant."

A local artist had his own style of art. He decorated his car. The car was decorated with plastic toys glued onto the surface of his car. There were dolls, dinosaurs, and toy soldiers on every surface. There were plastic fish, toy guns, tin space ships, and pieces of unrecognizable things. They covered nearly every surface of the car except for the windshield, lights and tires. There were so many things affixed to the car, the make and model were unrecognizable. It looked very interesting; however, it was impossible to tell what the car started out as.

Taking away what's not. As silly as it sounds, how do you get a picture of the *ekklesia*? You take the big bunch of ideas and practices that surround the *ekklesia* and take away all of those that are unnecessary. Or, you start removing all the ornamentation and extras so you can see what's underneath. So many things have been added to the *ekklesia* throughout the years, we can't recognize it.

Getting to "chairness." Here is where I'd like to ask you to take a little leap with me. You will probably not think that every "add-on" to the *ekklesia* is wrong. My point here is not to convince you of that. To understand what the essence of a thing is, we need to take away everything that is not necessary for its existence.

For example, to understand what a chair is, we need to strip it down to its basic elements. A leather, overstuffed rocking recliner is a chair, but so is canvas camp chair that unfolds from a little stuff sack. As children, we are presented the word *chair* repeatedly and match it up against different referents until we understand the idea of a chair. Essentially, a chair has a low platform which is about 19 inches high (or about 48 centimeters) on which one person can sit and has a back against which your back rests and is not affixed to anything. If we take away the back, you're left with a stool. If it is affixed to a bus or plane, it is a seat. If two people can sit on it side-by-side, it's a bench. Other parts, such as arm rests, numbers of legs, padding, etc., are variations to the idea of a chair but don't change the basic elements of what a chair is. To understand "chairness," we need to take away one thing at a time until we're left with just a chair.

In a similar way, let's start taking away what is not necessary for an *ekklesia*. If we can strip the *ekklesia* down to its essential points, we will be left with the clear essence of what it is: pure, distilled, unadulterated *ekklesia*.

Taking away the institution. What is an institution or organization? Interestingly, Miriam-Webster defines an institution as "an established organization or corporation." An organization is "an administrative and functional structure" and a corporation is "a body formed and authorized by law to act as a single person although constituted by one or more persons and legally endowed with various rights and duties including the capacity of succession." Both terms require a corporate structure and an organizational authority. There is a hierarchical structure. There is some paid person or group in charge. There are subordinate followers. There are rules for succession. There are rules for membership. A financial structure is necessary. There is a code of beliefs. Nowhere in the scriptures do you see the word *institution* – or even the thought of an institution – used to describe the *ekklesia* as such in any sense.

What does an institution bring with it?

- It can bring an allegiance to the institution rather than to God. Members of Churches may be proud of the fact that their father or grandfather started a particular Church or congregation. They may be more connected to the Church than to God.

- Allegiance to an institution brings a drive to preserve the institution even when it is terminally ill. Church members keep supporting a dying institution instead of looking for the living body.
- An institution brings with it extra-scriptural baggage. Some Churches are worried more about corporate organization and governance that they avoid the scriptures entirely. Or, it requires them to add appendages onto the institution/Church which make it unwieldy.
- Church members, when they look at an institution, look at what an institution or corporate body *can* do. "Just because you *can* do something doesn't mean that you *should* do it."[25]
- Those *cans* get tied to the institution and make it clatter and create drag on its real purpose. Appendages such as schools, day care facilities, recreation programs, elder care programs, publishing houses, missionary societies – which may be institutions owned by or controlled by Churches (institutions), are types of these *cans*.
- An Institution can also bring with it formal mergers, divisions, corporate conglomeration, affiliations, etc., that are all foreign to the *ekklesia* in both the universal and local sense.

What amazing thing we do see if we look closely: the *ekklesia* exists without being an institution. The closest thing we see as any type "organization" is when the *ekklesia* is described as an "organism," a human body. In Acts 2:47, the Lord added to their number, even though there was no "institution" or organization for them to be added to! It just existed.

Human rules. An organization or corporation also requires rules. Where do these come from? There are no rules for corporate succession or for corporate organization in the scriptures. If we make up rules, then we are adding to God's plan. Beginning in the fourth century, Churches organized themselves into hierarchies. Individual autonomy was surrendered to the Emperor as Christianity was made the "official" religion of Rome.[26] Once in place, even reformers couldn't see past the idea of the institution.

People believe that Churches require a set of beliefs to be agreed upon by the organization so that there will be unity. Who is so infallible that he

---

[25] It is almost as if Churches adhere to a law of quantum mechanics, Gell-Mann's Totalitarian Principal: "Everything not forbidden is compulsory."

[26] Some men had already started elevating themselves as single bishops or overseers who were over other bishops or overseers before Constantine arrived on the scene.

can create such a statement of beliefs? No human can. Our attempts to create these creeds and statements in reality *cause* divisions. Even the Nicene Creed shaved off splinters in the early church. One dissenter from the creed was banished by Constantine: if anyone taught his understandings, they would be under penalty of death by decree of emperor himself.

There is a myth that has been perpetuated generation after generation: if we are going to stay united, there must be some specific human statement of beliefs and acts that we all cling to. This belief was Constantine's motivation to call the Council of Nicea. He saw differences in understanding as a threat to the unity of the Church, and, therefore, a threat to the unity of his empire. The Nicene Creed was politically motivated. Books of Common Prayer along with common standard hymnals authorized by a governing board are also motivated by a perceived sense that centralized unity is necessary. Supposedly creedless Churches often rely on orthodox publishers to established their teachings, even if they are unaware of the process they put in motion. Such creeds and writings beg the question: Why do we need more than the scriptures?

A group may start denying creeds but eventually succumbs to creeds or standardized teaching. A college or a paper or a central "editor" becomes the de facto determiner of what is right or wrong within a group, even among groups that deny a central organization. Supposedly "creed-less" Churches will post a statement of what they believe (a creed) on their web sites, in their by-laws, handouts to visitors, member directories, or in their organizational papers if they hold property by a trust or a corporation. The Jehovah's Witnesses disavow creeds, but their teachings are regulated by their "Governing Body" which determines the correctness of their publications, and, therefore, they have a back-door creed. The Church of the Brethren professes to deny creeds; however, differences in understanding the scriptures are ultimately left to their regional district conferences. Disputes that are not resolved by regional district conferences are submitted to their Annual Conference. The minutes of the Annual Conference state their unified interpretation and becomes a de facto creed. The churches that sprang out of the Restoration Movement of the nineteenth century also disavow creeds. They are the Christian Churches, the Disciples of Christ, and the Churches of Christ.[27] Nevertheless, each of these groups' identities have been solidified through the decades by a set of unified beliefs which may or may not be specifically stated in writing.

Ironically, rather than unifying, human creeds divide.

Human hierarchies. In the scriptures, there is no distinction between "clergy" and "layman." The terms don't even exist there! That distinction came with Constantine when he institutionalized the church. He created a structure for it and centralized it with a proper Roman hierarchical organization. It is no wonder that the Roman Catholic Church closely resembles the empirical structure of ancient Rome. Later-formed Churches have instituted organizational structures that resemble the organizational trends of the time they were created. Churches created under monarchies, tend to have authority centralized in one person or small group. Churches started during democratic surges tend to have a democratic or republican structure. Still others tend to have a corporate structure with a board of directors, executive officers, employees, etc.

Other groups have created organizational structures to perpetuate their creeds. No such central organization or hierarchy existed when the *ekklesia* was first established. Originally, the many different *ekklesias* were like the individual tribes under the judges: each tribe was autonomous and did what was right "in their own eyes" or according to their own understanding. When the tribes wanted to impose a centralized structure, God said, "[T]hey are rejecting Me." 1 Samuel 8:7. When we set up human hierarchies and structures, we are rejecting God.

What about pastors, elders and deacons? Aren't they part of a hierarchy? No. The *ekklesia* is horizontal. Pastors (and elders) lead by walking in front of their flock: they must remember that they are part of Christ's flock, too. The flock follows voluntarily. Deacons are fellow servants. In the alternative, the *ekklesia* could be viewed as an upside down pyramid, with the elders or pastors and deacons being the servants and submissive to the flock. This will be discussed in the next chapter.

Paid pastors, preachers or speakers are add-ons, too. Paid orators were added to the Church by Constantine. Previously, when a man became an

---

[27] Whether or not you choose to capitalize c*hurch* in Church of Christ, there is no difference. When the majority take up the lower case "c," the lower case "c" then becomes part of an unwritten creed and identifying mark.

elder, he put aside his earthly work and lived in poverty so he could teach and care for the flock with all his attention. Yes! The job is that important The elders were the teachers. Although an Apostle or other teacher may have been passing through a particular area and spoke publicly to an *ekklesia*, preaching was not a regular part of the activities of the group. When Paul spoke until midnight in Troas, it was an extraordinary event. When you trace the travels of Paul and Timothy and the other early evangelists, they were itinerants, spending usually about 6 months in one place. And they were often *not* supported by the group they were working with, working jobs independent of the local *ekklesia.* For example, Paul was a tent maker. Even as late as 1897, it was recognized that a "hired pastor" was an addition to the *ekklesia* along with Church choirs, instrumental music, manmade societies and human devices to raise money to support the institution of the Church.[28] Paid orators just didn't exist originally. Evangelists existed, but they taught non-christians.

Superstructure. So where is this universal cooperation between the *ekklesias*? There was none. There is none. Just as the individual tribes governed themselves during the period of judges, so each *ekklesia* governs itself. Some may point to Acts 15 as precedence for a hierarchy, universal cooperation or a central authority. Nothing that was said in the letter to the Christians in Antioch, Syria and Cilicia was anything new: eating blood has been wrong since Noah stepped out of the Ark (Genesis 9:4), fornication has always been against God's ways (e.g. Genesis 9:20-25), and "abstain from things sacrificed to idols" is against worshipping any god who isn't the God (e.g. Exodus 20:3-4). Collective governance and unified efforts of *ekklesias* just didn't exist in the first century. *Ekklesias* individually sent money to other *ekklesias* through trusted messengers and sometimes used the same messenger. Individual *ekklesias* would "apostle" (send as a messenger or evangelist) a member to go strengthen or build up an other *ekklesia* for a limited time. Multiple *ekklesias* joining together for evangelistic efforts didn't happen.

---

[28] Daniel Sommer, *Octographic Review* , XL, October 5, 1897,1, as quoted by David Edwin Harrell, Jr. Ph.D., *Emergence of the "Church of Christ" Denomination*, 14.

Seminaries. If there is going to be superclass of paid clergy or orators, they need training and qualifications.[29] This supposition is dangerous on two levels.

First, seminaries and bible colleges dethrone God by their very existence. A seminary presumes that the scriptures are unknowable to common, everyday Christians. They imply that God is not wise enough, not intelligent enough nor capable enough to write a book that His followers can understand. Only one with special instruction can elucidate the Scriptures. This discourages individual Christians from attempting to understand the simple truth of the Gospel. People give up on feeding themselves. Because professional preachers, pastors, and clergy intellectualize the simple gospel pushing it beyond common people's grasp, "My people are destroyed for lack of knowledge." Hosea 4:6.

Second, Seminaries and Bible colleges emphasize – in a strange way – what is not. Here is how the cycle goes. A college needs to be accredited which requires qualified teachers. In order to teach at a college, a person must have a higher degree such as a Master's or Doctor's degree. To get an advanced degree in Theology, a person is required to study philosophies, theologies, various hermeneutics, and religions. Then, the teacher or professor brings back his or her baggage of all these false philosophies, theologies, hermeneutics, and religions back to the college classroom. When a class on the Bible is taught, the professor brings in the wide and varied teachings. Rather than just teach a subject or book, many different approaches to the subject are brought in. Because there can only be one right answer on examinations, students cannot reason for themselves: instead students must demonstrate their abilities to juggle the various theologies. They create Pharisees, people who learn teachings about teachings rather than learn the pure knowledge of God.

Where are the buildings? Early Christians met in various places, such as each other's houses daily! Acts 2. As soon as Constantine was "converted to Christianity," he began a building program to establish "Churches," elaborate buildings, that would be attractive for the common

---

[29] Learning Hebrew or Greek or other studies of the scriptures are not bad per se. We all need scholars who understand these things. Using such studies as a qualification for an "office" in the Church or to achieve a higher standing is wrong.

person and lure people inside.[30] Buildings dedicated exclusively as meeting places were extremely rare or nonexistent before that time. Christians met wherever they could. We know that the church in the first century met in people's houses: e.g. the house of Aquila and Priscilla (Romans 16:3-5 and 1 Corinthians 16:9) the house of Nympha (Colossians 4:15), the house of Philemon (Philemon 1:2).

When Saul was persecuting the *ekklesia*, he went from house to house arresting Christians. "But Saul *began* ravaging the church, entering house after house, and dragging off men and women, he would put them in prison." Acts 8:3. A notorious bank robber, Willie Sutton, was asked why he robbed banks: he said, "Because that's where the money is." Why did Saul go from house to house? Because that's where the Christians were gathered! Otherwise, he could have been more efficient by just going to their central meeting hall (if they had one) and rounding them up there.

Buildings are overemphasized. It's not that buildings are necessarily wrong, but they are a poor use of money. I know of a fund that was set up specifically to build church buildings throughout a former Eastern Block country even though there were not enough members of that denomination to half-way fill one small building let alone the number of buildings this group wanted to build. When an American missionary there refused to be a part of a plan to build empty church buildings, his monetary support was removed – this Church put that much emphasis on buildings. One Church had over a quarter of a million dollars sitting in its "building fund" while some of its members starved and no money was sent to preach the Word. Still others believe that worship only "counts" when group meets in a building. One young Christian met with a group that assembled in a house and was told by a deacon where he usually attended that worshipping with that group wasn't a real "Church" because they didn't meet in a separate building. Further, relying on buildings means huge expenses. Imagine what could be done for the cause of Christ if we could get along without buildings or at least with less lavish ones.

Can you have an *ekklesia* without a building dedicated for its use? Absolutely. As Jesus said, "...an hour is coming when neither in this mountain nor in Jerusalem will you worship the Father." John 4. Jesus was

---

[30] The English word *church* comes from a word meaning a large, often palatial building.

talking about being able to worship anywhere; even without a building! A building-less *ekklesia* may thrive better than one encumbered by physical property.

Social programs. I attended a meeting at a Church. It was held in a nice building with a kitchen and meeting rooms which was built for their Boy Scout Troop. Across the parking lot was a large modern building. It was very impressive. I complimented a friend on how impressive their Church building was. My friend corrected me: that was their elementary school. Where did they meet for worship? They met in a small metal shed that was in poor condition. They reasoned it was more important to have the social programs to reach out to the surrounding community. If they could attract people with programs, then people might start attending their Church. Some Churches exist solely to carry out social programs. Many Churches believe that organized sports teams or other types of entertainment are necessary to keep people connected to a Church. Does an *ekklesia* require schools, social programs, entertainment, and sports teams to exist? The clear answer is no.

Inter-church cooperation. Can an *ekklesia* operate on its own? Does it require other groups to survive or exist? How did it work in the New Testament? First there was the *ekklesia* in Jerusalem. Then, independent groups sprang up as Christians spread throughout the Roman Empire and beyond. We see throughout Paul's letters that individual *ekklesias* sent contributions to other *ekklesias*; we do not see *ekklesias* joining together into some coordinated effort. 1 Corinthians 16:3, 2 Corinthians 8:1-5 and 9:1-5, 2 Corinthians 8:1-5 and Romans 15:24. When an evangelist was sent, he either supported himself or was supported by the *ekklesia* that sent him. Philippians 4:10-16, 1 Corinthians 9 and Acts 18. They did not require a separate institution or organization to carry out the purpose of the *ekklesia*.

The *ekklesia*, in its purest form functions without the trappings and modifications that have been appended to it over many centuries. An *ekklesia* can exist without a building, without a creed, without other sister-*ekklesias*, and without a preacher. Clergy, seminaries, creeds and denominational hierarchies are ornaments that detract from the essence of the *ekklesia*. They entice the *ekklesia* away from its real goal and purpose.

11: A CLASSIC OR A HOTROD?

There are two way to look at a classic car that needs restoring. In the 1950s and 1960s if a car buff were to come across a 1932 Ford, chances are he would turn it into a hotrod or a customized car. These customized hotrods were memorialized in the Beach Boys' song "Little Deuce Coupe." The engines were removed and replaced with more powerful modern engines. The suspension and power train were replaced to accommodate the higher performance engine. The bodies were modified with more flared fenders and a lower profile. A custom paint job was a requirement. Ultimately, the Deuce Coupe would bear almost no resemblance to what was in the minds of the original Ford designers and engineers. So many 1932 Fords were modified, that unaltered models are now rare. Companies now produce fiberglass bodies and steel body parts mimicking those from 1932. A person finding an unaltered 1932 Ford today would most likely restore it to its original condition: it would be more valuable restored since so many people have destroyed their '32s by "improving" them.

The *ekklesia* designed by God has been customized so often that we recognize the Deuce Coupe versions more readily than the original model. The *ekklesia* might even be scoffed at because it doesn't contain all the additions that so many people find attractive. What do you mean it doesn't have .....? (You can fill in the blank.) Like an elegant, classic car, the beauty and ingenuity of the original can only be seen when the *ekklesia* is seen as it was originally constructed. Only then can we get a peak into the Designer's intention.

The foundation. We start with the foundation and cornerstone, Christ. Jesus Christ is the starting point from which everything and everyone is measured. Ephesians 5:20. Why is Christ so important? It is through Him alone that our relationship with God is reestablished. Because God is the source of life, being disconnected from Him means death. Our sins caused that disconnection. Because Christ cleanses us continually from our sins, He allows us to remain connected. He allows us to have that relationship with the Godhead. He allows us to have life. All things are measured against and aligned with Christ.

Christ's chosen Messengers (Apostles) are those stones that also form the foundation of the *ekklesia*. Revelation 21:14. Being witnesses of the Lord (Acts 1:21-22 and 1 Corinthians 9:1) and being inspired by the Holy Spirit, they revealed Christ to us so that our relationship with God can be reestablished. The knowledge revealed to them by Christ and the Holy Spirit resides in the scriptures. The reason Christ and the Apostles are the foundation is that they are the basis on which all our beliefs are anchored. Jesus did not say He was revealing truth: Jesus said He *is* Truth. John 14:6. Truth is what is necessary to overcome the stench of the lies of Satan. Remember, Satan's only real weapon is lies.

Getting back to our car analogy, Christ and the Apostles are the frame, suspension and drive train. They are the parts that hold everything together, onto which everything is fastened, and what makes it move. If the frame – the foundation – is bent or broken, the car will not function as it was designed. Hot rod enthusiasts found out that the front suspension from the Ford Mustang II (which was produced from 1974 through 1978) fits almost exactly on a 1932 Ford. So many people have "improved" their 1932 Fords that old Mustang II's are scarce: they've been cannibalized for their front suspensions. A similar thing has occurred in Churches. From the outside they may appear to be the *ekklesia*, but when you look at their foundation, they are founded upon human teaching, religious history and traditions, a board of governors, creeds or other philosophies. They are built on a foundation other than Christ.

Because the *ekklesia* is founded on Christ and the Apostles, it is the individual Christians who are affixed to Christ. What does that mean for the *ekklesia* as a group? It means that each Christian will understand some things the same as the others and will understand other things differently. Our relationship is with Christ first. He is the cornerstone from which all things are measured. When you see a genuine *ekklesia*, it will be filled with Christians who do not agree on everything. Their allegiance is to Christ and not to a Church or a Church's teachings. "So then, my beloved, just as you have always obeyed...work out your salvation with fear and trembling; for it is God who is at work in you, both to will and to work for *His* good pleasure." Philippians 2. Working out the details is an *individual* responsibility.

Living stones. Living body. Now comes the rest of us: living stones. By the rest of us, I mean anyone who is not Jesus or one of the Messengers. What is our part? What are we to do? How do the rest of us fit into the *ekklessia*? We are not left to guess our parts.

Paul sets out the various roles that people have in the *ekklesia*. In Romans 12:6-8, 1 Corinthians 12:8-10; 28-30, and Ephesians 4:11, Paul lists a number of gifts that have been given to Christians:

- Administration
- Apostleship (Messengers)
- Discernment
- Evangelism
- Exhortation
- Faith
- Giving
- Healing
- Interpretation of Languages
- Knowledge
- Leadership
- Mercy
- Miracles
- Pastor/Shepherd
- Prophecy
- Serving/Ministering
- Speaking in Languages
- Teaching

Christians have had these gifts and still have some of these gifts in varying degrees: Paul said, "I thank God, I speak in tongues more than you all." I Corinthians 14:18. The point of this book is not to argue for or against certain miraculous spiritual gifts today. The point is that we still have spiritual gifts. Some people are stronger in faith. I know a woman who abounds in mercy. Some people are very talented teachers while others are not. In 1 Corinthians 12, Paul emphasizes that we are all individual members of Christ's body with unique functions. Even today the Holy Spirit distributes the gifts to the body – the *ekklesia* – so that it is perfectly fit for what it needs to do:

And He gave some as apostles, and some as prophets, and some as evangelists, and some as pastors and teachers, for the equipping of the saints for the work of service, to the building up of the body of Christ; until we all attain to the unity of the faith, and of the knowledge of the Son of God, to a mature man, to the measure of the stature which belongs to the fullness of Christ. As a result, we are no longer to be children, tossed here and there by waves and carried about by every wind of doctrine, by the trickery of men, by craftiness in deceitful scheming; but speaking the truth in love, we are to grow up in all aspects into Him who is the head, even Christ, from whom the whole body, being fitted and held together by what every joint supplies, according to the proper working of each individual part, causes the growth of the body for the building up of itself in love.

Ephesians 4. The point is that the *ekklesia* functions as a body. Or, as God referred to it in the Old Testament "as one man." We let those who are gifted in administration, do the administering. We let those who are gifted in exhortation, exhort. We let those who can serve, serve. If there is a talent or skill needed to accomplish a work, the Holy Spirit will supply it. By doing so, we all grow. If we do not "one-another" each other, none of us grow. When each uses his or her gifts, we all grow spiritually and organically together.

Everyone actively participates. We have a glimpse into the functioning of that body. Paul continues in 1 Corinthians 14: "What is the outcome then, brethren? When you assemble, each one has a psalm, has a teaching, has a revelation, has a tongue, has an interpretation. Let all things be done for edification....But all things must be done properly and in an orderly manner." Notice that when the Christians assembled "each one" had a part in the assembly. It was not a few "worship leaders" or a choir or a preacher and a song leader. It was – and should be – "each one" that participated. The assembly of the body was not an orchestrated affair. Each Christian – each organ of the body – contributed to each other part so that growth occurred. The *ekklesia* in ancient Athens was a group where all contributed and actively participated. As the body of Christ, our actions are infinitely complex and require constant interaction of each part of the body being closely connected together and being intimately connected with the Head, Christ.

Most Churches do not function this way. A young Christian attended a Church service who had never attended or even visited a traditional Church of any kind. He had only met with Christians in their homes. The Church he visited was large and by most Church standards was a "very good" Church. When asked what he thought about his experience, he said you were told what to sing by a person with a big booming voice, a skillful speaker told you what to think and tried to make you have some emotional response. You had to sit quietly and never talk. You stood when they said and sat when they said. He said that he couldn't ask questions or talk to the person next to him to ask a question about a point. It was exactly what he thought it would be: a passive experience. That is completely opposite of the practices of the early Christians in which "each one" participated.

The shepherds. If one looks at the pastors or overseers of a Church, you will usually find men who are good in business and are considered to have some managerial skills. Sometimes they serve as the board of directors of a Church. They hire a preacher or "pastor" to feed and care for the flock. After all, these elders or leaders have businesses and lives, so they hire a minister to teach, visit the sick and to attend to the injured or those needing attention. Usually, the elders/pastors/overseers subcontract their work out to a minister/pastor, to a youth minister, or to another such person. This is not how it was originally. The work of an elder in an *ekklesia* is a duty that cannot be delegated to another.

Elders, overseers and pastors are the same thing. Acts 20. In the first and second centuries when men became elders, they often lived a life of poverty, giving up their own occupations and livelihoods to care for the flock among them. It is for this reason that Peter charged the elders in 1 Peter 5:

Therefore, I exhort the elders among you, as your fellow elder and witness of the sufferings of Christ, and a partaker also of the glory that is to be revealed, shepherd the flock of God among you, exercising oversight not under compulsion, but voluntarily, according to the will of God; and not for sordid gain, but with eagerness; nor yet as lording it over those allotted to your charge, but proving to be examples to the flock.

Instruction. Paul said that the shepherds should be appreciated because they "have charge over you in the Lord and give you instruction." 1 Thessalonians 5:12. Many forget how shepherds operated in biblical times and today in countries around Palestine. The shepherd walked in front, and the sheep followed. Just as Christ led and taught by example, so the shepherds or pastors walk in front, and the sheep –the members of the *ekklesia* – follow the pastors or shepherds.

This is contrary to the modern method of herding sheep in which a shepherd dog or sheep herder drive the herd from behind, pushing and prodding the sheep along. The shepherds of an *ekklesia* do not act in an authoritarian role. They do not "lord over" the flock. 2 Corinthians 1. This is contrary to modern thought: the leaders often rule by edict. That is herding sheep not shepherding

Care for the sheep. An elder/pastor/overseer told me that if a member were sick or failing, it was that Christian's responsibility to come to the elder. On the contrary when there is a sick or struggling sheep, the shepherd always goes to the sheep. How can this happen in an *ekkesia*? Only by each elder or overseer knowing the members of his flock *intimately* can true growth occur. This does not happen by a once-or-twice-a-week, casual "how are you doing." It is a constant, deliberate effort to know and to care for the other people making up the *ekklesia*. The shepherd should know when the sheep is sick before the sheep itself knows anything is wrong: the same was true for the elder-christian relationship. Why should it be any different today for us today? An elder's first job is to care for his fellow Christians from a knowledge of each member of the *ekklesia*. This personal knowledge arises from a close, personal relationship among and between each Christian in the *ekklesia*.

Servants of the *ekklesia*. Deacons are servants of the assembled Christians. They do this so that the elders only need to focus on spiritual matters. Acts 6. If the issue is something other than spiritual, it's the deacon's job. The elders should not be "waiting on tables" or in charge of anything physical, including money.

In many Churches today, the Deacons function as the pseudo-elders or elders-in-training. It often happens that the Deacons are the individuals who teach the members, especially the young. In other Churches, they act as the Board of Deacons and the misconceived rolls of Elders and Deacons are rolled into one to form a board of directors.

Where are the ministers? Call them what you'd like: Pastor, Priest, Preacher, or Evangelist. The problem is that in nearly every Church these public orators function as the Chief Executive Officer. Their names are put on the signs for the buildings. They write or supervise the publication of the Church bulletin or newsletter. They teach classes. They give prepared speeches once or twice on Sunday. They have "office hours." During the week, they are supposed to visit the sick. They plan the bible class curriculum. They visit the spiritually weak. In large portion, they are subcontractors for the elders and deacons to do their jobs. Often they are psuedo-elders. This is not how it should be.

In the first century, evangelists were rare. One *ekklesia* would send out, would "apostle," one or two of their own members to evangelize or strengthen another location. "How then will they call on Him in whom they have not believed? How will they believe in Him whom they have not heard? And how will they hear without a preacher? How will they preach unless they are sent?" Romans 10. The pattern is there. Evangelists preach to the unbelievers! On special occasions, they build up a work that has already been started. Today, preachers have taken over the responsibilities of the elders.

Imagine how this works and how many problems would be solved if we did things God's way. There would be no more preachers or missionaries looking for support. Men would not be going from Church to Church or to a Missionary Society looking for financing. A man from a his own *ekklesia* would be sent, apostled, as a messenger of the gospel for that *ekklesia*. This man would not be a stranger to the *ekklesia* because he would be one of their own. Also, because his *ekklesia* sent him, his success is their success, too. (Remember that all were not called as teachers. Not all were called to be apostles.) Each person would want to make sure that their apostle had everything he needed to spread the word. His failure would be their failure, too. Once the work was started, he would return home or go to the next location. Look at Paul's journeys: he would often leave an *ekklesia* that was started only after a few months. The *ekklesia* would also send their apostle back to check up on them and strengthen the group but only for a short time and never as a means of control.

Like a fine machine, God's ekklesia functions best when it is constructed and operated as its designers and engineers intended. The Body of Christ is a living entity with individuals uniquely gifted for the carrying out of its purpose. All work together with their own unique gifts. Elders must be the primary teachers and caregivers. Evangelists need to be apostles or messengers of the ekklesia rather than convenient subcontractors for the elders.

12: WHAT AN *EKKLESIA* IS

When a gemologist examines a precious stone to determine what it is and its value, he looks at it through a magnifying glass, a microscope, and may hold it up to the light. Some gemstones contain small inclusions that identify that stone uniquely. Some diamonds are etched with invisible identification numbers. The gemologist may also subject the gem to gas chromatography–mass spectrometry to determine its chemical make up. In a way, we have been examining a gem, too: God's *ekklesia*. It is the pinnacle of all creation. So what is this "thing" that God considers so valuable that He sent His own Son to die for? What is this "thing" that Christ considered so valuable that He was willing to suffer both physically, psychically and spiritually in order for it to come into existence. What is this *ekklesia*?

The *ekklesia* is not a Church. It is not centered around a building. It is not founded upon creeds and codes and teachings. The *ekklesia* does not have a hierarchy or large organizational structure. It is not an institution. The *ekklesia* does not create division by devising creeds. It is not a club or a social group or an instrumentality by which social programs or sports programs are administered. Membership in it is given by God, not voted on by humans. When we can say what it is not, we are in no way diminishing what it is. Something that the almighty God treasures above everything He has created.

An *ekklesia* is a Community. As we've seen how an *ekklesia* assembles, functions, and works, I hope it is obvious that *church* is a lousy word to describe it. A better word would be *community*. An *ekklesia* is a Community of believers. The Merriam-Webster dictionary definition of a Community is:

a. a unified body of individuals: as a state or commonwealth,
b. people with common interests living in a particular area,

c. an interacting population of various kinds of individuals (as species) in a common location,

d. a group of people with a common characteristic or interest living together within a larger society,

e. a group linked by a common policy,

f. a body of persons or nations having a common history or common social, economic, and political interests, and

g. a body of persons of common and especially professional interests scattered through a larger society.

All this fairly describes an *ekklesia*. Although this comes from an uninspired source and is not intended to describe the *ekklesia*, it coincidentally is an amazing description of what Christ established. Christ came to create a Community of believers. He came to establish relationships.

A unified body of individuals: a state or commonwealth. Christ came to established His Kingdom. What better description could there be of Christ's *ekklesia*? We are citizens of the Heavenly Kingdom. We have citizenship in a kingdom because that's where we were born. Psalm 87. We each seek for the betterment and improvement of our fellow citizens. Together we work for the building up of the body of Christ. We are the realization of the shadows of the Commonwealth and Kingdom of Israel. Christ prayed for unity among all believers, something it seems we've been wrestling with ever since.

People with common interests living in a particular area. That Christians have common interests is a given. We are seeking God and Truth. Jesus said, "For this I have been born, and for this I have come into the world, to testify to the truth. Everyone who is of the truth hears My voice." He also said, "I am the way, and the truth, and the life; no one comes to the Father but through Me."[31] John 14. As we search for that Truth, we are also being changed by the Holy Spirit. We are saved and sanctified by the Holy Spirit. 2 Thessalonians 2:13. God saved us by the washing of generation and renewing of us by the Spirit. Titus 3:5. Further, we are being led by the Spirit. Romans 8:14. As Christians, we have the common interest in that we are all sanctified and sealed by the Spirit. 1 Peter 1:2, Romans15:16 and 2 Corinthian 1:22. We have a common interest in

---

[31] Different from all religions where individuals claim to be revealing or teaching the truth. Jesus said He is truth. There is no separation between Jesus Christ and Truth or Jesus Christ and Christianity.

walking by the Spirit. Galatians 5. These are details of a larger point: our common interest is loving God and to be molded into His spiritual image. Our goal is to be like God and to be with God.

God's Community functions both universally and in small groups. Most Epistles begin with a salutation to the Community of Christians in a city or a region: "to all who are beloved of God in Rome, called *as* saints," "To the church of God which is at Corinth," "To the saints who are at Ephesus," etc. Even when he addressed a book to a province, Paul addresses it to the individual Communities in a region: "To the churches (*ekklesias*) of Galatia." This shows that there were Communities of believers in various cities in the region. From the Book of Acts and from the letters themselves, we know that the Christians were in the minority, and, therefore, were a Community of people with a common interest living in a particular area and within a larger population of nonbelievers..

An interacting population of various kinds of individuals (as species) in a common location. As we sit around with a group of other Christians, we see people. However, God does not see us as merely people see because God looks at our hearts. 1 Samuel 16. God sees a new species – new spiritual creatures. 2 Corinthians 5:17. We are a "new creation." Galatians 6:15. We are different from all the human creatures that are around us. Paul emphasizes that we are a different race in his first letter to the Community at Corinth: "Give no offense either to Jews or to Greeks or to the church [*ekklesia* or community] of God...." 1 Corinthians 10. We are neither Jews nor gentiles. Earlier in the letter Paul made a distinction between the Jews, Greeks and "those who are called." 1 Corinthians 1. Usually, the Jews made a big distinction between the Jews and non-Jews, considering them two races of humans. Now, under Christ and through the Holy Spirit, a third race has been created. Christians are that new creation, that new spiritual species of being. We have been "renewed." This happens through Christ and the Holy Spirit. Through Christ we have the washing of regeneration. Through the Holy Spirit we have the renewing or our minds. Titus 3:5. When a group assembles together, we could call them a community. When these individuals – this new species of spiritual beings – gather, they are a Community. I wish I could see ourselves as God sees us: not a group of flawed individuals struggling to survive and to exist together. He sees us as blameless and spotless. He sees us as His most beloved children, the beautiful bride of His Son, and the dwelling place or temple made of gem stones and pure gold. The anxious longing of all creation waits with unspeakable eagerness for us, the children of God, to be revealed. At the writing of this book, my daughter is expecting my first grandson: I am eagerly waiting for him to be revealed. Perhaps our attitude would be different if we saw each other as God and the spiritual beings see us. All creation is almost breathless just to know who we are.

A group of people with a common characteristic or interest living together within a larger society. The Community of Christians should be separate from the world. While we are in the world, we are not of the world. John 15. We struggle to escape the desires of the flesh and to produce the fruit of the Spirit. Galatians 5. Pierre Teilhard de Chardin described our existence quite accurately: "We are not human beings having a spiritual experience; we are spiritual beings having a human experience." As Christ prayed that we might be one just as He and the Father are one, He was emphasizing that all Christians have common characteristics and traits – not just common with each other, but common with the Godhead. Those common characteristics and traits make us different from the society around us. Paul quoted God's urgings for us to come out from the world: society at large:

I will dwell in them and walk among them;
And I will be their God, and they shall be My people.
Therefore, come out from their midst and be separate…
And do not touch what is unclean;
And I will welcome you.
And I will be a father to you,
And you shall be sons and daughters to Me.

2 Corinthians 6. We are in a larger society, the world, from which God wants us to remove ourselves: "come out from their midst and be separate." We have been cleansed so we are to keep ourselves "unstained by the world." James 1:27. Christians are separate and unique. We have common characteristics in that we have "put on Christ" and are "conformed to His image." Romans 8:29 and 13:14. This makes us a Community, a group of people with a common characteristic living in a larger society, the world.

A group linked by a common policy. All true Christians everywhere live by several very simple principles. Foremost, Jesus said, "A new commandment I give to you, that you love one another, even as I have loved you, that you also love one another." John 3:34. James expressed our religion, our common policy, in simple terms: "Pure and undefiled religion in the sight of our God and Father is this: to visit orphans and widows in their distress, and to keep oneself unstained by the world." James 1:27. We have other things we do together: but if they were listed, each one would fall into one of these simple categories: loving God above all else, loving our neighbor as ourselves, and remaining unstained from the world.

Beyond this, we all have the same attitude toward "things," whether it's money or possessions or houses. We have no attachment to them. We know "the love of money is a root of all sorts of evil." 1 Timothy 6. We know that because everything on this earth will be destroyed with intense heat, we place no value on them: we concern ourselves rather with "holy conduct and godliness." 2 Peter 3. Our citizenship transcends our physical citizenship: I have more love and commonality with Christians in other countries that I do with my fellow citizens in the nation where I was born.

A body of persons or nations having a common history or common social, economic, and political interests. We are very much like ancient Israel in that we have a common history of being freed slaves. We were once slaves to sin. Romans 6. And as ancient Israel was freed from bondage when they were "baptized" through the sea, so we, too, were all freed from bondage when we were baptized. 1 Corinthians 10. Christians are all members of the same kingdom, regardless of their physical nationality. We belong to a kingdom "not of this world." John 18:36. "Our citizenship is in heaven." Philippians 3:20. As citizens of that heavenly kingdom, we all have a common knowledge of Yahveh, our God. Hebrews 8:11. We are a Community of nations. Genesis 28:3. Our social interests are to care for others. Our political interests transcend the ephemeral politics of the day and region in which God has placed us. We should love our fellow Christians regardless of their politics. I have worshipped with conservative, right-wingers as well as devoted Marxists. The political views of our fellow believers should mean nothing to us. A Community of believers transcends politics.

A body of persons of common and especially professional interests scattered through a larger society. Christians come from all walks of life and from all professions. Some of us are poor. Some of us are rich. As varied as we are in physical interests and professions, we are united in a single profession. Spiritually, we are farmers and fishermen. We are the reapers bringing in the harvest that is white. John 4. We are the "fishers of men" as the Apostles were. Matthew 4:19. We are all fellow workers in the kingdom of God. Romans 16, 1 Corinthians 3:9, 2 Corinthians 8:23, Philippians 2:25, 4:3, Colossians 4:11, Philemon 1. We can join in the work by supporting those who we "apostle" into the world. 3 John 8. What is our profession? Reflecting the Light into a dark world.

God describes the *ekklesia* as a Community, as a kingdom and as a nation. A "people for God's own possession." God's Community of believers interacts with one another in a locality. We all have a common heritage as slaves who have been redeemed and set free. We all have a common perception of and attitude toward things physical and spiritual. As citizens of God's Community, our heavenly citizenship transcends nationalities, international borders, nation politics and individual philosophies.

PART FIVE: BEING AND DOING

TOM MANN

13: CHRISTIAN NUDIST COLONIES

Several families I know have started raising chickens for eggs. There is a great satisfaction in knowing what the chickens eat, how healthy they are, and, therefore, how pure the eggs are. Keeping chickens also requires vigilance. If a chicken is hurt or has a bloody spot, the other chickens will start to peck at its wound. Farm supply stores sell a medicine that is a blue color to hide the red blood and to help the chicken heal. If the flock continues pecking at the wound, the chicken will die. The same thing happens too often in Churches. Christians see a small flaw or bit of blood on another in the flock and peck it to death. They pick, peck and poke at the flaws of another until that person spiritually dies.

How do Church members avoid being pecked to death? How does it work in Churches?

Pretending. One answer is to pretend. There is a wonderfully appalling poem that describes so many church goers, "A Beautiful Young Nymph Going to Bed" by Jonathan Swift. The poem describes a "beautiful" woman preparing to go to bed. As the poem progresses, she removes her wig, makeup, her teeth, her glass eye, etc. In truth, her "beauty" is an artifice that she applies each day to hide her flaws: in reality she is a disease-ridden prostitute. Many Churchgoers do the same. On Sunday, they daub over whatever problems they may have. Eyedrops can hide bloodshot eyes from a night of drunkenness. A pot of strong coffee and a roll of mints can keep one awake through almost any sermon. They appear on time at the right places. They wear the right clothes. They hide their sin to avoid being judged for their weaknesses. So they figuratively and literally make-up their faces covering flaws, wearing a suit and tie or Sunday morning dress. Because their only connection with other Christians is at the Church building, their hearts and their deep troubles are unknown. Church changes nothing for them. As one person said, "Christians are just like everyone else; they're just busy on Sunday."[32]

Still, others have doubts and struggles. The common thought in Churches is that if one has doubts or struggles, they are spiritually weak. The opposite is true: questioning is part of the search for truth. Struggling is part of our spiritual lives. If we are not struggling with something, then we are doing something wrong. Satan doesn't have to mess with those who are already in his camp. But, if we speak of or reveal our doubts and struggles in Church, we will be marked as weak or as one not holding to the faith. In reality, all should be questioning and struggling. Failing to admit that Christians doubt and struggle leads to just charges of hypocrisy by the world. Perhaps those with the most questions are the stronger Christians.

Self-beautification. Another way is to make ourselves "beautiful" to other Churchgoers. Some people avoid being pecked by doing the "right things." If they attend each Sunday worship service and Wednesday bible study and attend all the potlucks, group meetings and social gatherings, then they must be good Christians. These people teach the right classes from the right workbooks or have their lessons from the right workbooks filled out in advance. No one wants to show weakness. Many churches "take roll" so they know who is consistently present and who has a "good excuse." Others may make themselves attractive by being "good givers" – meaning their check in the collection plate is significant enough that the elders overlook sins as differences of opinion. Or, they give in other ways, such as writing cards or bringing food. Please note that I am not saying that meeting with fellow Christians and giving is wrong. I am saying that some do it as a way to make themselves appear good to avoid scrutiny. Jesus condemned the Pharisees who did these same things so that others would see them for their good works.

Along with looking good by acts, is looking good by dressing right. This attitude may not be everywhere, but it is so prevalent that there is a pattern. One young man struggled to get his four children to worship services while dealing with a wife who had a debilitating disease. He showed up slightly late and the children were not spotless. The young man received one word of "encouragement" that day from a woman in the Church: he needed to

---

[32] *Beware of Christians* (Riot Studios, 2011), Will Bakke, director.

bring his children to Church in neater and cleaner clothes. I know young men who were chastised for not wearing a tie on Sunday morning. Women who wore pants to church were placed on a second tier from those who exhibit more spirituality by wearing dresses. Even members of Churches who pride themselves in saying that they are accepting in what people wear have declined to let men "wait on the table" because they weren't dressed "right." I know a man who had no clothes to wear other than shorts and a T-shirt who was being encouraged to attend a Church service: "Nobody cares what you wear there," he was told. In describing how openminded that Church was, the Church member said that one Sunday morning someone wore khaki pants and a shirt without a jacket or tie! The poorly clothed man did not "go to Church" that morning.

Hiding. Still another method to avoid the life-robbing pecking is to hide. One man told me once during a layoff period where he worked, "They can't fire me if they don't know I'm here." Many people in churches take that approach: they just hide. They attend quietly. They do not get involved. They find very large churches. They move from Church to Church. Often they keep to themselves. The Churchgoers just leave them alone thinking that they just must be quiet people. However, they may have deep troubles and disturbances in their lives. They believe God is the answer and that He can be found in Church. From experience they know that if they open up, they will be looked down on, considered weak or strange, and be ostracized. So they try not to be noticed. In conclusion, they may get something from being in the surroundings, but their deepest needs are not met.

How it works in God's Community. Why do we hide behind clothes, rote acts, and facades? We fear being judged. That's what happens in a Church. That is *not* what happens in a Community: there is no fear in love. 1 John 4:18.

Judging fellow Christians is contrary to what being a Christian is all about. Jesus said, "Do not judge, and you will not be judged; and do not condemn, and you will not be condemned; pardon, and you will be pardoned." Luke 6:37. Christ also said it another way, "Do not judge so that you will not be judged. For in the way you judge, you will be judged; and by your standard of measure, it will be measured to you." Matthew 7:1-2.

We can see Paul trying to get the local Community in Rome to put Christ's teachings into practice. What was their problem? They judged each other:

> Therefore you have no excuse, every one of you who passes judgment, for in that which you judge another, you condemn yourself; for you who judge practice the same things. And we know that the judgment of God rightly falls upon those who practice such things. But do you suppose this, O man, when you pass judgment on those who practice such things and do the same yourself, that you will escape the judgment of God?

Romans 2:1-3. "Who are you to judge the servant of another? To his own master he stands or falls; and he will stand, for the Lord is able to make him stand." Romans 14:4. Then Paul says,

> But you, why do you judge your brother? Or you again, why do you regard your brother with contempt? For we will all stand before the judgment seat of God...So then each one of us will give an account of himself to God. Therefore let us not judge one another anymore, but rather determine this—not to put an obstacle or a stumbling block in a brother's way.

Romans 14:10-13. Someone reading Romans 14 might say they were judging each other over matters of opinion. This is true and not true: for the people who were observing a religious day or eating certain foods were doing so out of conscience and conviction that those acts were the right things to do.

Confessing without condemnation. James said, "Therefore, confess your sins to one another, and pray for one another so that you may be healed." James 5:16. How do Churchgoers get this done?

Some go in private to confess to a preacher, elder, priest or pastor; however, the confession is one way only. Some Churches carry on the tradition of the mourner's bench, and come forward at the end of a sermon during the altar call or invitation. Many times the confessions are for nebulous sins, wrongs, or weaknesses. Those who have the courage to confess publicly, are often judged or considered weak, sometimes banned from participating in Church activities until – as in the words of one Church member – they've "repented enough." An elder told me that one young man who had committed adultery and repented shouldn't be participating publicly in the Church for a while: it just wouldn't look right. What could be more touching than the prayer of a tender, repentant soul? "Lord, forgive me, a sinner?" The Church too often values the Pharisee's prayer over the tax collector's. Luke 18.

Worse, we're marked for life. A preacher's wife once called a woman asking if a mutual friend had committed adultery. The woman said that yes, she had, but that she had repented and reconciled with her husband. The preacher's wife's response was, "And I thought she was a good Christian." It appears that this repentant Christian had been demoted from the ranks of "good Christians" to just "mediocre Christians" or, worse, to "bad Christians." I was unaware that such a hierarchy existed.

This pattern is contrary to the way God's Community functions. Paul and James both tell us how to confess. But, so many of us are buried in the Church traditions, we overlook how God's Communities worked – how they are supposed to work *now*.

Trespass trap. Before we get into the confessing part, let's look at how to deal with the sin part. In Galatians 6, Paul said,

> Brethren, even if anyone is caught in any trespass, you who are spiritual, restore such a one in a spirit of gentleness; each one looking to yourself, so that you too will not be tempted. Bear one another's burdens, and thereby fulfill the law of Christ. For if anyone thinks he is something when he is nothing, he deceives himself.

How do we react to a fellow Christian in a sin? With a spirit of gentleness. Why? Because we, too, can be tempted. Our response to our siblings' sins? To help them bear the overload. To help them discontinue the sins. The last caution is not for the person caught in the trespass, it is for the one who is spiritual: "For if anyone thinks he is something when he is nothing, he deceives himself." God here warns us against our own tendency to compare sins: ours versus theirs. He warns us that when we see faults in other people, we tend to think we are better than they. Christians are all sinners and are all covered by God's grace: no one is greater than another.

Now take this attitude that Paul expresses and apply it to what James said: "Therefore, confess your sins to one another, and pray for one another so that you may be healed." James 5:16. We read this a lot, but we fail to read it in context:

> Is anyone among you suffering? Then he must pray. Is anyone cheerful? He is to sing praises. Is anyone among you sick? Then he

must call for the elders of the church and they are to pray over him, anointing him with oil in the name of the Lord; and the prayer offered in faith will restore the one who is sick, and the Lord will raise him up, and if he has committed sins, they will be forgiven him. Therefore, confess your sins to one another, and pray for one another so that you may be healed. The effective prayer of a righteous man can accomplish much...My brethren, if any among you strays from the truth and one turns him back, let him know that he who turns a sinner from the error of his way will save his soul from death and will cover a multitude of sins.

This passage is often looked at concerning someone who is ill. Notice the connection between the suffering and the sins! There is a connection between suffering and prayer. Notice the mutuality or the reciprocity of the actions here: confess to one another and pray for one another so that *you may be healed.* This is both a physical and spiritual healing. Notice the result of our mutual prayers and confessions: we can save a sinner and "cover a multitude of sins." Whose sins? Both theirs and ours. What is happening here? This is a spiritual version of "one hand washes the other." If we all mutually acknowledged our weaknesses to each other, without judgment or condemnation, what would be the result? Both of us would be stronger. I would pray and help strengthen you with your burden. You would pray and help strengthen me with my burden. This only comes about through confessing our sins and then supporting one another in "saving a soul from death," which just may be our own.

What happens when we acknowledge our sins? We acknowledge our Savior! When we acknowledge our sins and that we have been forgiven of them, we rob Satan of his taunts. The movie, *One Nation Under God*, begins with four young college men introducing themselves. One says, "My name is Lawson Hopkins. I'm a Christian, and I've made more mistakes than you have." Another says, "My name is Will Bakke. I'm a Christian and a hypocrite." When a certain relatively new Christian would accidentally say a curse word at work, his coworkers would say, "And I thought you were a Christian." This new Christian's response would be "I am, and who needs a savior more than me?" They were speechless. Satan is completely disarmed when we acknowledge our sins and acknowledge the saving blood of Christ that is washing us clean.

...and without license to continue. Paul says it succinctly, "Are we to continue in sin so that grace may increase? May it never be!" Romans 6. Just because we confess does not mean that we can just continue to do the same sins repeatedly.

There was an incident when everyone thought Jesus gave sinners a pass, but He did not. There was a woman who was caught "in the very act of adultery." The Pharisees brought her to Jesus to test Him: "Now in the Law Moses commanded us to stone such women; what then do You say?" John 8. The reaction of Jesus makes many people believe He refused to enforce the Law of Moses: that He gave the woman a "free pass." The opposite is true.

It appears that this woman was set up. First, where is the man? In Deuteronomy 22:22, both the man *and* the woman were to be killed. Jesus was in the middle of teaching publicly in the Temple. A large group of men brought the woman to Jesus: the scribes and the Pharisees as a group interrupted Jesus's teaching by throwing her down directly in front of Him. Such a large group of men was unable to produce the male sinner as well? More likely, the male adulterer was in league with the scribes and Pharisees: and the woman was purposefully caught so they could try to trap Jesus. These scribes and Pharisees prized embarrassing and discrediting Jesus over the life of this woman. They persisted and taunted Jesus, demanding that He condemn this woman to death.

Instead, He forced the Pharisees to "confess." After they persisted, Jesus told them, "He who is without sin among you, let him be the first to throw a stone at her." Now, who was the person to cast the first stone? Moses said that it should be the witnesses. "The hand of the witnesses shall be first against him to put him to death, and afterward the hand of all the people." Deuteronomy 17:7. Jesus forced these scribes and Pharisees to acknowledge their own sin in the situation: they were as culpable as the woman. Then Jesus turns to the woman after her accusers left: "Did no one condemn you?" She said, "No one, Lord." Jesus admonished her: "Go. From now on sin no more."

Christ's first lesson here is that confessing our sins to one another makes us compassionate and merciful to one another. What saved the woman was confession which brought mercy. When they were confronted with their own sin and forced to confess in a way, even the murderous Pharisees showed mercy.

His second lesson is that once we confess our sins, we should not "continue in sin." As Jesus told the woman and many other people throughout His ministry, "Go and sin no more."

Confession. Mercy. Encouragement. Accountability. What is the conclusion to all this confessing? First, we realize that we are all weak – each one of us. When we hear our brother or sister confess a sin, we show them mercy, because we, too, have sins. We encourage each other to cease from sinning. Last, it makes each one of us accountable to the others in the Community to become more spiritual. We encourage and edify without giving another permission to keep doing wrong. When the pattern of sinning turns from weakness to willfulness, then we may need to discipline. Otherwise, what is our reaction when that same person might confess that same sin again? Compassion, mercy and encouragement.

Back to the garden. Back to the Community. When Adam and Eve were in the garden and in a sinless state, they were naked and unashamed. They were in a perfect Community with God. Once they sinned, they tried to "hide" their sins with their own stitched together apron of fig leaves to artificially maintain that Community. When confronted with their sins, they were afraid. God clothed them with animal skins: a sacrifice, blood and death, covered their nakedness. Christians need to let God do the same for them.

We need to live our lives shamelessly and without fear. Although we should not glory in our shortcomings, we should live a life acknowledging our sins. At the same time, we acknowledge the magnificent grace poured on us without measure. Acknowledging our sins doesn't make us look better or worse. (Trying to look better to others is a carnal matter motivated by fear and by "the pride of life.") Acknowledging our sins glorifies God and His forgiveness: His compassion is glorious beyond comprehension. Acknowledging our sins simultaneously acknowledges God's mercy and love to the world.

In order for the Community to function as God intended, we need to allow God to cover our sins with the blood of His Son. We have no reason to live in fear. Although we acknowledge sin, we know that Christ's blood covers *all* our sins, even those we haven't committed yet. Ephesians 1.

Then, we can confess our sins, but also see each other as God sees us through the lens of the blood of Christ: holy, blameless and without flaw. There is no need for shame or guilt. There is no reason to hide. There is no reason to pretend to be someone we are not. There is no fear: perfect love casts out all fear. A suit and tie or Sunday dress doesn't cover our sins. Nor are we clothed in the skins of animals. We are clothed in the white robes of the saints. Not earned, but given to us as a gift by God.

It is amazing how powerless the foe becomes when we acknowledge our sins and praise God that He sent His Son to cover them. When we see ourselves as God sees us, where is there the tiniest flaw or spot for another in the flock to peck?

In a Community, people freely acknowledge their own shortcomings, weaknesses and sins. No one compares sins more or worse than any other. Christians do not judge each others, but encourage and love without giving license to continue in sin. Each member know that every member of the Community is cleansed by Christ's blood and saved by God's grace and not of their own works.

14: BECAUSE WE EXIST, WE HAVE HELP

When I was in college, a hand-me-down car was a magnificent blessing. As a poor student, I couldn't place a value on it. I was in law school and prohibited from working during the school year by the school rules. So when my in-laws gave us their thirteen year old Volvo 140 series sedan, it was a blessing. We were ecstatic to have it. Being a very basic sedan, it had little in its favor except for a radio, air conditioning and reliability. It had no accessories: I mean that literally. It had a manual transmission. It did not have power door locks. It did not have power windows. It did not have power brakes. Worst of all, it did not have power steering. As a teenager I occasionally drove a 1948 Chevrolet dump truck when I was working for my dad. The old truck was a huge challenge to drive. The ancient dump truck drove like a fine luxury car compared to that old Volvo.

Decades later, God has blessed me with a nicer car. My car now has all kinds of accessories that help me drive it. There are buttons that adjusts my seat and mirrors. The brakes are "power assisted" and are antilock so they help me to stop more easily and safely. The car senses when the tires slip and strategically applies the brakes to keep me from skidding. The doors lock automatically when I start driving. My lights come on automatically so I don't forget. The air conditioner and heater come on automatically and either heats or cools as necessary. My windshield wipers will come on exactly when the windshield gets too misty. The rearview mirror darkens when a car behind has its lights on too bright. The car has a lot more devices that help me drive it. So many of these helps just work, and I never realize they are happening: I often forget. Newer cars have even more helps than my eight year old car. Nevertheless, after driving that old Volvo, the single thing I appreciate most is the power steering.

Power steering is a mystery to me. If I need to turn right, some magical, mystical hydraulic system engages in the engine and makes it easier for me to turn right. Now I would understand if it worked in only one direction or the other: but it helps turn both left and right. If I happen to be passing a truck during a gusty day, the power steering helps me stay straight and relatively unaffected by the wind. Although it helps me maneuver the car, it does not steer it for me.

When you think about it, none of these conveniences in our cars *drive the car for us*. They make it easier for us to drive. We still must determine our speed, direction and, ultimately, our destination. So it is with the life of a Christian. We are surrounded by myriads of helps. "Helps" is one of the gifts given to Christians. 1 Corinthians 12:28. Speaking of the Father, Paul said, "For assuredly He does not give help to angels, but He gives help to the descendants of Abraham." Hebrews 2:16. We are surrounded by so much help that we sometimes forget that we are being helped: things can seem to happen automatically.

Catastrophically, in our lives we ignore these helps and attempt to live our lives alone – solo – without any help. In a sense, we disconnect the power steering, power brakes and everything else meant to help us wrangle life. This self-sabotaging behavior frustrates us and makes us feel isolated. When an animal is isolated from its herd, it is most likely to fall to a predator.[33] When a Christian is separated from her "flock," she is the most vulnerable to the enemy. The enemy is going about the earth seeking who he can devour. Job 1:7 and 1 Peter 5:8. Who in the flock are the easiest prey? The young, the sick, and the isolated. There is purpose in the words we sing as we plead in Psalm 119:176, "Seek me who like a sheep has strayed."

Satan wants us to feel alone. He doesn't want us to sense the help we have as we "steer." He wants us to reject the help we have and say, "I've got this all on my own." It's also tragic that those Christians who say, "I can handle this by myself," are those who are often put in leadership positions as preachers, teachers, evangelists, pastors, elders, bishops and deacons. Seeing themselves in control, they trivialize, ignore or deny their

---

[33] The film *Never Cry Wolf* (Walt Disney Productions, 1983) is a good dramatization of the idea that predators seek out the young, old, weak, and sick of the herd. It is ironic that Satan's efforts actually strengthens God's kingdom by weeding out the weak of the flock!

weaknesses and reject help. Tragically, those persons suffer often from the most hypocrisy, the largest egos, and, when they stumble, crash from elevated heights. Their falls often disillusion, discourage and drive away believers.

Alternatively, Satan wants us to feel out of control. He wants us to feel as if we are careening and spinning alone and disconnected from all the help we have. Abandoned. Deserted. Discarded. Stranded. Orphaned. Disconnected. Isolated. Unplugged. It is amazing that many Churches treat fellow Christians who have committed a sin – particularly one they view as a public or notorious sin – as discarded, stranded, orphaned, disconnected, isolated and unplugged. They do this to them when they are most vulnerable. They "help" them by attempting to sever them from all help that a struggling brother or sister may need to return to the Christ. After speaking to Christians who have been disciplined by having all help withdrawn from them, I know the opposite effect results. How much sense would it be to pull a life preserver away from a drowning swimmer when it is just barely a finger's length away? That is what we do to drowning Christians weekly.

Heeding the whispered lies. However, feeling alone and isolated is in reality a matter of perception. In the Broadway musical *Spamalot*, King Arthur sings, "Each one of us is all alone. So what are we to do, in order to get through. We must be lonely side by side. It's a perfect way to hide." This sentiment pervades society generally and many Churches. If we think we are alone, we are believing a lie that originates from the deepest pits of hell. We are never alone. We have comfort and assistance that originates from the Creator of all that is. We have assistance from the Creator of the universe because that assistance fulfills His own supreme purpose for creating all that exists. The Creator wants to help us, because His assistance provides what we need to accomplish the ultimate culmination of His creation, the pinnacle of all creation and of all His love: us, His Community.

Because we exist, we have help. Many people think that a person receives help because of some good thing they've done or because of some debt another person owes. In the movie, *The Avengers*, two characters talk about doing good deeds because they have "red ink in their ledger." However, Christians are justified: there is no red ink. At the same time, we are "in the black" not as a result of our own doing. The whole idea of being owed help or being a debtor who must give help is completely foreign to godliness and Christianity. Our mere existence as Christians means that we have help beyond our wildest comprehension. Just because we exist as God's children – as His Community – God helps us. This needs to be repeated: our very existence means that God helps us. We have a wealth of help because we have a wealth of relationships. Our help comes purely from God's lovingkindness. Our help comes through His grace. This is part of God's plan for our existence. Metaphorically, each Christian's life is a drive in a luxury car with more than all the imaginable assistance needed to assist us on our journey. It's a shame that many Christians figuratively disable all the automatic helps and then feel frustrated because they're having to struggle with everything alone.

Our help comes in many forms. This book is about God's Community. As I am writing this, my heart aches because I cannot talk more about the Father, Jesus Christ and the Holy Spirit. I feel like a newlywed trying to write my first anniversary card and running out of space on the greeting card to express my love, devotion and appreciation. But, in this chapter we need to look at how each of these forms of help interact with the individuals of the Community.

God the Father. The Source. The Father is the source, the fountainhead of the plan for us. He is the one who forgives us of our sins. Mark 11:25-26. The Father is the source of life and our necessities. John 5:26. Matthew 6, 7, 18. The Father is the source of every spiritual blessing and of all spiritual wisdom and knowledge. Ephesians 1. We know that Christ submitted Himself to the Father so that the Father's great plan could be effected. In turn, as Christ submitted Himself to the Father, so the Father gave Christ all authority. As Christians, we abide in Christ and the Father. John 17. God the Father is the source of our blessings, both physical and spiritual. He is the answerer of prayers. Matthew 18:19. As heirs of the Father, He is the source of our inheritance, the Kingdom of God. Matthew 25:34.

Even more amazing, is that because we have Christ, we also have the Father: we abide in Him! 1 John 2:24. 2 John 2:9. Because He is our Father, we can cry out to Him and know that He will hear us and answer our requests. Galatians 4:6.

Jesus. Our Savior. Our Redeemer. Our Mediator. Jesus is one of our helpers. Do not be disillusioned by thinking that Christ lived, suffered and then died for us and then just left us alone. "And Jesus came up and spoke to them, saying, 'Go therefore and make disciples of all the nations, baptizing them in the name of the Father and the Son and the Holy Spirit, teaching them to observe all that I commanded you; and lo, I am with you always, even to the end of the age.'" Matthew 28. Look at what Jesus said to us! "I am with you always, even to the end of the age." This was not a promise just to the apostles: this is a promise to us, too, because we are living through the end of the age. Jesus said He would not abandon us as orphans! John 14:18.

At this point in this book would be an appropriate place to insert a description of all Jesus Christ has done for us. Just contemplating what could be written teases our thoughts into depths that no human mind can comprehend. As John said, "Jesus did many other things as well. If every one of them were written down, I suppose that even the whole world would not have room for the books that would be written." It is standing on a precipice looking at once into a bottomless pit while at the same time staring with deep clarity into the highest heights of space. What Christ has done for us, we cannot fathom. However, from the scriptures, we can get a glimpse into what He has done and is doing for us now. Jesus Christ is the one who took on condemnation for our sins and reconciled us to the Father. Through His scourging we are healed. Through the blood of Christ, we are now holy, sinless and blameless. He continues His role as High Priest making propitiation for our sins. Hebrews 2. Because He was tempted as we are, He is sympathetic to our weaknesses, and, therefore, He intercedes for us to the Father. Romans 8, Hebrews 4 and 1 John 2.

When it comes to the Community, He is the Head. He is the King. He is the Word. If we look for other heads or kings of the Church among men, we dethrone our Lord. If we look for other authority than Christ alone, we strip Him of His sovereignty. When we try to improve or clarify the Word through creeds and the teachings of men, we veil the Word with distorted stained glass and diminish His glory by twisting His image. We take the pure, clear Word of God and adulterate Him with human thought.

The Holy Spirit. In the first century during the Roman empire, there was hardly a person more neglected and abandoned than an orphan. With no mother, father or family member to protect or provide for them, orphans were almost certain to be left with a life of utter poverty. When Christ was speaking with his disciples, He assured them that they would not be abandoned as orphans. We have even more help: we have the Holy Spirit. Jesus said,

> I will ask the Father, and He will give you another Helper, that He may be with you forever; that is the Spirit of truth, whom the world cannot receive, because it does not see Him or know Him, but you know Him because He abides with you and will be in you. *I will not leave you as orphans.*

John 14. (Emphasis supplied.) Jesus didn't promise the Holy Spirit just to his Apostles because the Holy Spirit is with us forever. How wonderful is that thought!

The Spirit dwells in our hearts, the seat of our emotions and thought. We know that the Spirit intervenes for us in our prayers. There are times when our words cannot express what we feel: our Helper, the Spirit, takes over and expresses those things for us. He is the *paraclete*, the advocate or the attorney, who speaks for us when we are speechless and when words fail. As an attorney who speaks on our behalf before a judge, so the Spirit helps us by advocating on our behalf to our Mediator, Christ.

The Spirit leads us into truth. Purposefully, He dwells in our hearts: our emotions are often our largest impediment to our renewal and regeneration. He softens and molds us and transforms us. Notice in Romans, Paul said "And do not be conformed to this world, but be transformed by the renewing of your mind..." Notice that *conforming* is something we do: *being transformed* is something that is done to us. It is the work of the Spirit. Titus 3: "[Christ] saved us...by the washing of regeneration and renewing by the Holy Spirit whom He poured out upon us richly...."

Concerning the Community, the Spirit is the one who unites us all: we were all baptized into one Spirit. As a Community, it is the Spirit who is building us collectively into a Temple, a dwelling for God. Ephesians 2:22. It is through the Community that we "preserve the unity of the Spirit." Ephesians 4:3. As each Spirit-filled Christian (1 Corinthians 3:16) comes together with other Spirit-filled Christians, we are reassembling the body of Christ and reunifying the Spirit. Through the Community, through the reuniting of the Spirit and the assembly of the body, we have encouragement, consolation, fellowship, affection, compassion, peace, joy, service, edification, purity, kindness, and genuine love. Philippians 2, Romans 14, 2 Corinthians 6. He also gives us gifts so that the Community, the Body of Christ, is fully equipped to fulfill God's mission. 1 Corinthians 12.

There are several cautions God gives us regarding the Spirit. First, we can quench the Spirit: if we fail to listen to Him or observe the paths He has set before us, we intentionally lose God's assistance. 1 Thessalonians 5:19. Others grieve the Spirit by their sins. Why would you upset someone who is solely determined to help you? Ephesians 4:30. Still, many deny that they have the Spirit of God in them. They do so at their own peril: those who do not have the Spirit within them, do not belong to Christ. Romans 8:9.

Angels. Remember the frightened servant of Elisha when he was in a city and surrounded by the army of the King of Aram? The servant was terrified by the sight of so many soldiers. But Elijah prayed that the servant's eyes might be opened and "see that those who are with us are more than those who are with them." 2 Kings 6:16. When Yahveh opened his eyes, "behold, the mountain was full of horses and chariots of fire all around Elisha." 2 Kings 6:17. What the servant could not see initially was the help God provided: myriads of angelic spirits ready to assist. For we know that angels are "all ministering spirits, sent out to render service for the sake of those who will inherit salvation?" Hebrews 1:14. As inheritors of salvation, we also have myriads of angels at our disposal to help us. Unfortunately, we just don't "see" them.

Let's look back at how the angels have helped. When Christ was suffering after His temptation by Satan and when He prayed alone in Gethsemane, the angels came and strengthened Him. Matthew 4:11, Mark 1:13, and Luke 22:43. When Peter was in jail, an angel opened the prison doors and led him out to safety. Acts 12. How do angels help us today? In more ways than we know and in ways we do not understand. We do know that the purpose of their existence is to help us! They are there, even though we, like Elisha's servant, do not see them. Never discount those powerful servants. When you see God's purposes being fulfilled in your life without rational explanation or with seemingly, inexplicable cause, praise God. We do not know by what means or which of His servants He used.

The scriptures. It is sometimes too easy to get lost in the physical battle of this world. I pity the misguided souls of the middle ages who equated the battle of sword and shield against the "infidels" with the real spiritual battles that Christians endure daily. Those poor souls sought physical battles without realizing that our actual war is "not against flesh and blood, but against the rulers, against the powers, against the world forces of this darkness, against the spiritual forces of wickedness in the heavenly places." Ephesians 6:12.

Realizing that we are not engaged in a physical battle should also make us realize that our instruments of warfare are not physical. When all is said and done, the war we are engaged in is a war between the truth and lies. When we look at the "full armor of God" Paul describes in Ephesians 6, there is only one offensive weapon: "the sword of the Spirit, which is the word of God." In other words, the Truth. We see Christ using this "sword" repeatedly, silencing the Scribes and Pharisees and forcing Satan to flee. When Christ was tempted by Satan, He overcame by the truth: "it is written."

Since the creation of humans, our battle has always been a battle between seeking the truths of God and swallowing the seemingly easy lies of Satan. Beginning with Adam and Eve, humankind has almost consistently chosen the easy path of lies. The Lord God told them that if they ate of the tree they "shall surely die," and Satan lied to them and said, "you shall not die." The same conflict between truth-and-life and lies-and-death exists to this day. This deadly conflict continues even at the very instant you are reading this sentence.

Our foe, Satan, however, has a limited arsenal of weapons. We know his schemes. 2 Corinthians 2:11. Satan is the Father of Lies. John 8:44. We know from 1 John 2 that all Satan's weaponry centers on our three weaknesses: the lust of the flesh, the lust of the eyes and the pride of life. The basis of each one of those weapons is founded in one way or another upon lies.

Ultimately, what is the Word? It is the Truth. Jesus said that He is Truth. The Truth gives us power. If we know it. If we know Him.

My fellow passengers. As a young driver, I used to get angry when my wife or a friend would point out that a light had just turned yellow or that someone was stopping abruptly ahead of me. As I matured and after some narrowly missed collisions, I've learned to stop saying, "I see it. I see it." Now I say, "Thank you for pointing that out." My wife and fellow passengers have saved me from tangles of bent metal, broken glass and loss. Our fellow believers – our fellow passengers – are blessings; they are helps we don't take advantage of. Let's talk about them next.

As a Community and as individual Christians, we have help from divine sources. We are not orphans. The help surrounds us, embraces us, and inhabit us. All these helps are waiting eagerly for us to use them. We just have to ask without doubting, and help appears. That is what makes a Community a unique creation in God's universe.

15: A HEAP OF ONE-ANOTHERING

Point your finger at something right now. This is probably about the simplest activity you can do. What did it take for you to do that simple task? This is my simple understanding. Your eyes worked together to collect light: pupils dilated or contracted to give you the right amount of light while your lens focused for an optimal view. Nerves sent these impulses to your brain to make sense and "see" the object. Your inner ear sent impulses to your brain so that you could tell which way your body was oriented and coordinate what you saw in relationship with your body. Your eyes worked together to let you sense how far away the object was. Nerves in your muscles sent impulses to your brain so you would know the relative position of your arm, hand and finger to your body and the thing you are about to point to. Then, an impulse was sent from your brain down a system of nerves instructing some muscles to tighten and some to relax. Because your finger muscles are connected to your circulatory system, blood supplies fuel and oxygen for your finger muscles to contract. This fuel came by way of food that was chewed with your teeth and jaws, swallowed by a complex system of muscular contractions and put into your stomach where precise acids broke down the food into usable compounds. Then these were absorbed into your blood through your intestines. Your blood also flows through your lungs and picks up oxygen needed for you to use the fuel. The amount of fuel and oxygen in your blood is constantly monitored and adjusted so there is not too much or too little. All this blood is flowing because your heart is constantly pumping the blood to all parts of your body at the right rate and pressure. The fuel, oxygen and nerve impulses work together: your finger points at the object. But, this simple action also produces some waste, which the blood automatically collects and disposes of. The carbon dioxide is exhaled through your lungs when you breathe out and the other compounds are filtered through your kidneys and liver, both of which constantly monitor your blood for impurities and waste. You just pointed at something. Simple, right?

A community is more complex. As Christians today, we live in an interconnected environment which is infinitely more complex than the human body. If God made our bodies (as well as the rest of creation) so complex and ingenious and the entirety of creation was made as an expression of God's greatness, then the process of our salvation is unfathomably more complex and greater. Even though we don't see things happen spiritually, complex, interrelated processes happen nonetheless. When it comes to the Body of Christ, the Community, the interrelationships are critical to our functioning and survival: the Community is described as a body, as Christ's body. The Community is described as a growing body:

> ...but speaking the truth in love, we are to grow up in all aspects into Him who is the head, even Christ, from whom the whole body, being fitted and held together by what every joint supplies, according to the proper working of each individual part, causes the growth of the body for the building up of itself in love.

Ephesians 4:15-16. We are all part of Christ's body, perfectly fitted together for whatever need may arise. Each one of us has a unique purpose in that Spiritual body of Christ. 1 Corinthians 12. In order for growth to happen – whether individually or as the entire body of Christ – the Community must function together.

Going it alone. A severed finger cannot point. Why? Because it is not attached to the complex system of a body that allows it to be used, nourished, replenished, heal and grow. It is dead or shortly will be. A Christian trying to live outside of a Community is like that severed finger: he is very limited in what he can do. He is almost useless.

My wife has a very good set of knives in the kitchen. We use them daily. Through daily use, they become dull. There is no such thing as a self-sharpening knife. My son-in-law will come to the house and sharpen them using steel and a honing block. Solo Christians are the same way. Alone, life dulls them and they become less and less useful. Solomon set out this principle: "Iron sharpens iron, So one man sharpens another." Proverbs 27:17. Associating with other Christians makes us sharper. Other Christians make us *and* them more useful in God's kingdom. If you are trying to go it alone, you are depriving another Christian of his or her growth. Solo Christians dull themselves and other believers.

While writing this book, NFL quarterback Tim Tebow was released by the New York Jets and was a free agent for a time: he was a quarterback without a team. Although it could be argued that he is a good football player, Tebow had no team to be a part of. Many Christians are similarly adrift and unattached. They know more of what they don't belong to than what they do belong to. Many Churches – I would cautiously say most Churches – do not supply the genuine needs of individual Christians much less the Body of Christ. So there is no need to become part of a "Church team" because the Church does not supply their needs. Therefore, many Christians are naturally disillusioned by Churches but have nothing else to attach themselves to. This dilemma reminds me of the agony of a character in a movie who desperately wants to belong to an organization and sobs, "I have nowhere else to go! I have nowhere else to go!" Then there are others who become so lifeless, emotionless and disconnected, they just "go it alone." They are flying solo. They become sort of spiritual "free agents" unattached to any "team." Eventually, they become that quarterback with no one to throw to. They become dull knives. They become that severed finger that exists but doesn't function. This also is not how the Community functions.

It's in the whistle. During World War II scientists were developing radar. There was a problem with efficiency: they needed to create a signal strong and stable enough while using a small amount of energy. They were stymied until they came across a simple answer in a simple device: a whistle. Using the model of a whistle, John Randall and Harry Boot invented the cavity magnetron.[34] The multiple cavities in the device amplifies the microwaves. When the scientists applied this simple whistle principle electronically to radar, they were able to increase the device's efficiency and make a stronger signal while using less energy.

When Christians do the things of God with other Christians, the same principal applies. A single Christian is like a weak whistle. It works, but just not as efficiently. Involve another Christian in your work, the effect of your work will become "louder." The more that are added, the effectiveness of the work is increased beyond just simple addition.

---

[34] The microwave oven in your house probably uses this device!

One-anothering. God put us all together for a purpose. We are here to help each other through this life and to persevere on to heaven. As each person helps the next, and then the two help two more, the one-anothering grows at a geometric rate. As it grows, the acts of caring for each other creates bonds between the members of the body that are strengthened more and more as the body functions. Paul said,

> "...but speaking the truth in love, we are to grow up in all aspects into Him who is the head, even Christ, from whom the whole body, being fitted and held together by what every joint supplies, according to the proper working of each individual part, causes the growth of the body for the building up of itself in love."

Ephesians 4. Notice that "every joint" is necessary for the proper working and growth of the body. There are no unnecessary organs in the Community. Each individual Christian has a place in the Community, supplying something that is unique to him or her. Otherwise the Community does not grow. Otherwise the individual Christian cannot grow.

Love. The primary thing we should do for one another is love. This is so important, that Jesus said it was a new commandment: "A new commandment I give to you, that you love one another, even as I have loved you, that you also love one another." John 13:34. This single command that we Christians love each other echoes through the scriptures. John 15:12,17, 1 John 3:11, 23 and 2 John 1:5. This is not a casual, see-you-in-church kind of love. This love is supposed to be sincerely fervent: "Since you have in obedience to the truth purified your souls for a sincere love of the brethren, fervently love one another from the heart...." 1 Peter 1:22: "Above all, keep fervent in your love for one another, because love covers a multitude of sins." 1 Peter 4:8. The word *fervent* comes from the idea being hot, boiling over, and greatly intense. How do you experience and give this intense kind of love? God teaches us how to love each other: "for you yourselves are taught by God to love one another..." 1 Thessalonians 4:9. The love we have for each other originates from God Himself and is manifested by His expressions of love. 1 John 4:7, 11. As we continue in love, God causes love within the Community to grow even greater, to abound and to be made complete. 1 Thessalonians 3:12, 2 Thessalonians 1:3 and 1 John 4:12. That fervent, expanding, absolute love (which is a reflection of Christ's sacrificial love for us), should shine through us so that people will know that we are Christ's followers: "By this all men will know that you are My disciples, if you have love for one another." John 13:35. Ultimately our love for our fellow Christians should approach the same love we have for God and that God has for us: a perfect triangle of love that grows indescribably. God loves me. I love God. I love my fellow Christian. As the love flows between and among us, it does not lose its power. It is amplified, magnified, and perfected as it saturates us. Psalm 133.

Greet with kisses. Arising from that fervent love are demonstrations of it. One such demonstration is a kiss. In North America and many European countries, a greeting with a kiss just doesn't happen. Personally, I believe non-kissers miss out. Four times in the scriptures we are *told* to greet each other with a kiss. Romans 16:16: 1 Corinthians 16:20: 2 Corinthians 13:12: 1 Peter 5:14. Some people substitute a hug for a kiss. I have been blessed to worship with brothers and sisters in other countries who take this practice literally. I was uncomfortable at first: I even tried hiding in a back corner at the end of worship. Eventually, then I got used to it. There is great wisdom here. When we kiss a fellow Christian on the cheek, all pretenses and animosities are either revealed or just melt away. It is difficult to kiss another when problems lie between you and the other person. Greeting with a kiss can reveal a little subconscious problem that things need to be fixed. Alternatively, it may just reinforce that wonderful bond between Christians. After a week or two, it will seem natural. Each person in the Community should try to or be willing to kiss every other member: young and old, male and female. (If you're skittish, at least try giving a hug.)

Service. The Lord Christ was our great example of service. I can hardly imagine the Creator of all there is and the King of kings, kneeling before a group of common men and washing their feet. Afterward, He explained that we should give each other the same kind of service: "If I then, the Lord and the Teacher, washed your feet, you also ought to wash one another's feet." John 13:14. Love for one another compels us to serve each other. Galatians 5:13. As we have received gifts from God, we are commanded to "employ" that gift to serve each other. 1 Peter 4:10 and 1 Thessalonians 5:15. Loving God, fellow Christians and the rest of the world provides us with a special constant quest: "....but always seek after that which is good for one another and for all people." 1 Thessalonians 5:15. All the while we are serving each other, we need to be vigilant to find ways to stimulate each other to good works and even more love. Hebrews 10:24. Beyond this, we also should serve the needy and downcast of the world. James 1:27. No task should thought to be too menial or too disgusting.

Subjection. Another attitude that comes from loving and serving each other, is humility. We put our fellow Christians before ourselves. "Do nothing from selfishness or empty conceit, but with humility of mind regard one another as more important than yourselves..." Philippians 2:3. We are to be humble towards each other. "...Clothe yourselves with humility toward one another..." 1 Peter 5:5. I have listened to preachers rail that a wife must be subject to her husband quoting Ephesians 5:22 while omitting the verse just before: "and be subject to one another in the fear of Christ." Ephesians 5:21. Submission is an honorable thing. Christ submitted Himself to the Father even to the point of death. Philippians 2:8. Growing out of Christ's example of love and service is submitting myself to everyone else.

Tolerance. As we learn to love, serve and submit to one another, a strange byproduct arises. We become more tolerant of our fellow Christians and live in unity. We do not judge each other's weaknesses or faults. We don't put obstacles in their way back to God; rather, we exist to encourage others to grow toward Him or to return to Him with humility, kindness and love. Romans 14:13. Paul implores us "to walk in a manner worthy of the calling with which you have been called, with all humility and gentleness, with patience, showing tolerance for one another in love, being diligent to preserve the unity of the Spirit in the bond of peace." Ephesians 4. After reminding us to preserve the unity of the Spirit, he reminds us that there is *one* body. That body, the Community, is supposed to live in unity as Christ prayed that night in Gethsemane. By not obstructing nor judging each other, we help make unity a reality. "Therefore, accept one another, just as Christ also accepted us to the glory of God." Romans 15:7.

Unity of mind. Being one body, we are also to function together with one mind. Paul said that if we, individually, are proud and think of ourselves as wise, we destroy that unity by consuming each other. "But if you bite and devour one another, take care that you are not consumed by one another. Be of the same mind toward one another; do not be haughty in mind, but associate with the lowly. Do not be wise in your own estimation." Galatians 5:15.

There are two diseases that these spiritual conditions are similar to in a physical body. Turret's syndrome is a disease in which the body does things that the person's mind doesn't want it to do. It results in twitches, spasms, and verbal outbursts. A Community that is not unified in mind will act the same way. An outsider looking in will see confusion, lack of coordination, and complete dysfunctionality. On the other hand, pride among the members of the body acts like an autoimmune disease, such as rheumatoid arthritis, where the body attacks itself and has crippling results. When members of the Community act haughtily and feel intellectually superior, the body is in the process of rejecting its members – eating itself up – and, therefore, stops working properly.

Encourage and edify. Hardly anything makes a young child feel better when playing a sport than to hear cheers of encouragement coming from his or her own team and parents in the crowd. The Community should function the same way: we are all team members cheering each other along. 1 Thessalonians 5:11 and Hebrews 3:13. We are thoughtful in how we stimulate one another to love and good deeds. Hebrews 10:24. Because each person is motivated and encouraged by different things, we need to make sure we motivate and encourage each other in meaningful ways. By encouraging one another, we are imitating God: "Now may the God who gives perseverance and encouragement grant you to be of the same mind with one another according to Christ Jesus." Romans 15:5. We encourage because God encourages.

We don't just do this on Sundays! Hebrews 10:25 says we are not to forsake "our own assembling together." The word "assembling" is also translated "gathering" in 2 Thessalonians 2:1. The writer is talking much more than just a weekly gathering for a "worship service":[35] he is saying that we need to "gather" or "get together" often to encourage each other. These "gatherings" or "get togethers" are described in Acts 2: "And day by day continuing with one mind in the temple, and breaking bread from house to house, they were taking their meals together with gladness and sincerity of heart, praising God and having favor with all the people." This is exactly what Peter was talking about when he said that we must "be hospitable to one another without complaint." 1 Peter 4:9. The Community gathers

---

[35] The term *worship service* is not found in the scriptures.

frequently for unity and encouragement. When you are with other people that frequently – almost daily – you cannot help but feel devoted to one another in love and honor. Romans 12:10. What is the result of all this fellowship and hospitality? "[I]f we walk in the Light as He Himself is in the Light, we have fellowship with one another, and the blood of Jesus His Son cleanses us from all sin." 1 John 1:7

The byproduct of our encouraging and building each other up is peace in the Community. As we encourage, we esteem and love each other for the work that is being done. Peace and harmony result from that encouragement. Peace and encouragement are two forces that mutually drive each other. Romans 14:19 and 1 Thessalonians 5:13. As I encourage and edify you – and you, me – we create an environment hostile to animosity and dissension and fertile for peace and harmony.

Care. As we are molded into one mind and as we act as one body, we begin caring for each other. Just as a person would massage her sore feet, or a finger would remove a fleck of sand from an eye, the Community cares for itself. As a single unified body, each member or part of the body cares for the other parts: "So that there may be no division in the body, but that the members may have the same care for one another." 1 Corinthians 12:25.

When I was young, I thought I could pick up anything without paying attention to how I was doing it. So I'd just bend over and pick up a heavy object without thinking about my back. After hurting my back several times, I learned to "lift with my legs." I used my legs to make up for what my back could not carry on its own. The same principle applies in the Community. We are to "bear one another's burdens." Galatians 6:2. The word "burdens" here is really "overloads." My back couldn't lift the weight by itself, so I enlisted the use of other parts of my body that could. In the Community, we are so interconnected, each member knows when a burden is too much for him or her and the other members of the body step in to help out, often without being asked. After all, God helps us even when we don't ask Him for help. Why should we act any differently?

With the maintenance of the body, also come care for parts or members that are injured or weak. Digging a splinter out of a finger may be slightly painful even when we do it ourselves carefully, but it's removal is necessary for the healing of that part of the body. At times, the weakness or sin is not so obvious: that is why we are commanded to "confess our sins to each other." I knew a person who was very ill, but would not tell anyone about her cancer symptoms until it was too late for her to recover. Confessing a sin or weakness is the first step toward healing, a process in which the whole body participates. As James said, "...confess your sins to one another, and pray for one another so that you may be healed." James 5:16. The sooner confession is made, the quicker the healing begins. The healing of the whole body.

When a member of the Community is weak or in sin, we lovingly take care to heal that part of our body: "...you yourselves are full of goodness, filled with all knowledge and able also to admonish one another." Romans 15:14. We restore – heal – the member of the Community with love and gentleness. Why? Because when we sin, we will be cared for and restored in the same way! Galatians 6:1. There is a basic knowledge that each of us is human, and we will all sin or will offend one of the other members of the body eventually. For this reason, we must be quick to forgive each other. Ephesians 4:32 and Colossians 3:13. Tenderhearted forgiving is part of our new spirit in Christ. Again, we forgive because God forgives. We are tenderhearted, because God is tenderhearted.

Singing. Have you ever depressed the damper pedal on a piano and then struck one note very hard? If you listen carefully, you can hear other strings start to sound at the same time even though they weren't struck: they vibrate with the other strings because they are "in tune" with that note. If you have the lid of the piano open, you can feel the vibration of the other, unstruck strings.

Another interesting experience is hearing Buddhist monks chant the "ohm" sound in an echoing room or cave. One chanting by himself is interesting. Twenty-five or thirty monks humming in sympathetic, complementary tones which echo back and reinforce the chant is a spine-tingling experience.

When Christians sing the "Word of Christ" (Colossians 3), a similar experience should occur. The unity of words, thoughts, emotions and tones should make each soul – each component of the Community – vibrate sympathetically with each other soul. Because the Community sings the Word of Christ, God's Word dwells in us richly, and we are filled with the Spirit. Some scholars have suggested that Ephesians 5:19 refers to the practice of one part of the Community singing a phrase and the other repeating it: "speaking to one another." That verse and Colossians 3:16 are often taken out of context, being used to emphasize singing in a formal assembly. The contexts have nothing to do with corporate worship! This is just what Christians do. We sing. Early Romans were trying to figure out this new "cult" and described Christians gathering before dawn to sing. They described Christians singing to each other while they worked in the fields. Fishermen sang as they mended their nets. Singing together is just what the Community does...and not just on Sundays and Wednesdays!

Alone or with a team? How do you handle a bully who is bigger, stronger, smarter and more skilled in fighting than you? If he were a human, I'd run. If I had people or police to help me, I'd call them in. Otherwise, I'd be helpless. But, I can't run from Satan. Satan is stronger than I am. Satan is smarter than I am. Satan has been fighting with people much longer than I've been alive. So, I'm not going to run. I'm not going to give in. I'm going to get my helpers to defeat the bully. As we talked about earlier in this chapter, I have a gang of fellow Christians all banded together "as one man" or as "one body." I have an untold number of angels whose sole purpose is to help me. But most importantly, I have God. Christ has already taken on this bully and rendered him powerless. Satan is powerless that is, if we resist and use our helps. With them, our mere resistance makes the cowardly bully run away. James 4:7.

Besides defending ourselves, there is one more reason to work together. With our fellow Christians and with our help from God, we can accomplish anything. Paul said, "I can do all things through Him who strengthens me." Philippians 4:13. "Nothing is impossible with God." Luke 1:37. But, also remember what God said about the power of people collectively: "Behold, they are one people, and they all have the same language. And this is what they began to do, and now nothing which they purpose to do will be impossible for them." Genesis 11. Imagine what we could do for God if we were all unified.

Christian joining together in a Community set off a chain reaction of mutual love, care, fellowship, encouragement, discipline and teaching. They create bonds tighter than any physical family. a primary purpose of the Community is the mutual help we have from each other. All this "one-anothering propels us towards our Creator.

16: THE BODY IN ACTION

Paleontologists can learn fascinating facts by looking at fossils and footprints left in rock. One set of fossil footprints meandered through the exposed stone in Arizona's Painted Desert. The paleontologists determined which extinct dinosaur made the prints based on skeletons they had discovered. They could tell from the size of the footprints the approximate size of the animal and, therefore, the size of the legs. Then they measured its stride. From these set of facts, they came up with a fairly good idea of how fast the extinct animal was running when it made those tracks.[36] Although some might think that a living, breathing Community is extinct (although it is not), from the footprints left in the Scriptures, we can "see" God's Community walk and move in all its grace and beauty.

Shoulds and shouldn'ts. Someone posed the question, "Is God a legislator or an artist?" When we view God as a legislator, all we see is law. As a result, men turn the scriptures into an elusive set of "shoulds" and "shouldn'ts." They view God's Words as if it were a statute book. "The written Law kills..." 1 Corinthians 3:6. If we see God as an artist, we will see beautiful pictures and stories. However, He gives us pictures of His purpose: to reconcile us to Him. In reality, God is both. As a legislator, God's laws reflect His nature. He reveals who He is and how we are different from – or fall short of – God. As an artist, God paints a picture of what He wants us to look like. So let's marry the two to get the full picture.

So, what's a Community? First, its not an organization. God's Community is a collection of relationships. When we are reunited with God through Christ, He adds us to His Community: no membership dues, classes to pass or applications to be made. God puts us in. Then, we have relationships with fellow Christians who have the same relationship with

---

[36] See http://www.sorbygeology.group.shef.ac.uk/DINOC01/dinocal1.html, retrieved June 17, 2013.

God. Have you ever had the experience of meeting someone for the first time with whom you have a mutual, close friend? There is often an automatic connection between the two people. A similar thing happens when we encounter other Christians: we've just found a long-lost relative that we never knew we had. The Community brings us into an instant relationship with other Christians. It is as though we have just found a close relative we never knew: after all, we are adopted children into the same family.

A Community is made up of relationships between people who have a common relationship with God.

Next, a Community is very active. Because of our relationship, Christians form close bonds in which we do things for and with one another to make us stronger. We carry one another's burdens. The Community works together as a body, as "one man." When the Community gathers together, each Christian actively participates. When we all are acting as a body, each Christian employs those Spirit-given gifts to move the Body of Christ into action. As God said, "Behold, they are one people...and now nothing which they purpose to do will be impossible for them." Genesis 11. We can bring realization to what God said.

A Community acts as "one person," so that when we are joined together in a common bond, nothing is impossible for us.

We have no shame, guilt or pride in our Community. We do not judge: we exhort. The Community is where we "let our hair down" and give up all pretensions. We know that we have all sinned, but we also know that our sins have been purged by the blood of Christ. Because God sees us as clean and spotless, we see each other in the same way. Acknowledging specific sins to our Community does not create fear: we know that we will be encouraged and loved, but never judged. Our confessed sins puts a spotlight on God's forgiveness of those sins. We are humbled, and God is glorified. Because God does not judge us, we do not judge our fellow Christians. A man said that Community meetings should be like an Alcoholics Anonymous meeting. This may be a good analogy except for the "anonymous" part. There is no need to be anonymous because Christians do not judge. We embrace our sins. Think of God's people whose sins became part of their name: Rahab the Harlot, Matthew the tax collector, etc. The sin in their names point to and acknowledges God's grace and mercy. We know who God is. We acknowledge that we are forgiven and listen to others' confessions. And we know that we are powerless to "fix" ourselves. If others judge us for our forgiven sins, it reflects their weakness and immaturity.

A Community is a group of interdependent people who freely confess their sins to each other and strengthen each other in love. By recognizing Christ's continual cleansing, they (1) have no fear (because perfect love casts out all fear), (2) use their confessions of sins to strengthen each other, to reflect Christ's mercy and compassion and (3) have an even greater cause to glorify our God and our Savior.

In a Community, the elders/pastors know each member of the Community personally: they know their flock so well, they may even know of a Christian's problems before the Christian does. The elders do the teaching: they do not subcontract any of their responsibilities. The elders or pastors may sacrifice their own careers and all their resources for the spiritual care of the members of the Community. At the same time, the elders are not overbearing dictators. They function in the same way that Christ led his disciples, with patience and by example.

A Community is taught by its elders, ensuring that each individual is growing and maturing. The elders lead by example and not by edict.

A true Community sends out and supports its own members as "apostles" to carry the gospel to the world. They commit to supporting their evangelist as he goes out to convert others. That work is a local or long distance extension of the Community's work. There is no "minister" or "preacher," because the elders/pastors/shepherds do the teaching. When the elders do their job as given to them by God, a local minister or preacher becomes obsolete and redundant. His job would be to go where he is sent and teach in other places or possibly in the community in which he lives.. He would an evangelist in fact and not in title.

The Community "apostles" or sends its own members to evangelize other cities and towns. Their apostle is not afraid of being unsupported, because his own family, his Community, sent him.

How does a Community get together? The first Community started with a group of three thousand and later rose to five thousand or more. Acts 2 and 4. But, where did they gather? Although they had a location where they could assemble – a least right at first – it appears they met daily in each other's houses. Why is this important? It is important because they met more frequently with each other than just once or twice on Sunday. They met with each other daily. Acts 2. Although they initially gathered in the Temple courtyards, that venue was most likely lost as the Jewish leaders persecuted them. So they began meeting house to house. As previously noted, that's why Paul went from house to house rounding up Christians to persecute. Acts 8. Notice the references in Paul's letters as to where the Community met: the house of Mary (Acts 12), Prisca and Aquila (Romans 16 and 1 Corinthians 9), the house of Nympha (Colossians 5), Philemon's house (Philemon 1). They also met in other public places such as the "lecture hall" of Tyrannus. (Acts 19) There is archeological evidence of a large room used for worship in a home that would accommodate about fifty to seventy people. As late as 303 A.D. evidence shows that Christians continued to meet in houses. At that time Emperor Diocletian ordered the Christian Scriptures confiscated and burned. In Cirta, the capital of Numidia, the police went first to "the house where Christians used to meet."[37] When Christians went to synagogues on Saturdays, it appears that Jewish Christians did so attempting to convert their Jewish countrymen to Christianity and not as a location for a meeting place for the Community. See Acts 17:1-2, 17:10, 18:4, 18:26, and 19:4.

---

[37] See *Corpus Scriptorum Ecclesiasticorum Latinorum*, xxvi, pp. 186-8 as quoted by Bruce M. Metzger in *The Canon of the New Testament: Its Origiin, Development, and Significance*, p. 107.

The early Christians met mostly in homes and rented halls in smaller groups, even when there were large numbers in the city. They met often and informally. They met in groups that were small enough that they could know each other very personally.

The Real Sense. *Community* conveys the meaning of *ekklesia* better than *church*. Looking back to the Nation of Israel, we see them first described as a Community when they stopped acting like a crowd of disparate persons and started acting as a unified group or as a community. One person commented that the *ekklesia* was "a body of Christians called out of the Roman and Judean system[s] to come together into a separate civil community." In other words, Christians were both called *out of* their physical communities and called *into* a new spiritual community.

One more thing. Where are the non-Christians in God's Communities? They are not there. Too often we look at Church services as evangelistic opportunities. "Invite your friends to Church." We do this expecting the preacher to teach them for us in sermons. These thoughts are holdovers from nineteenth century tent meetings. A Community meeting is for the Community itself. Personal teaching of non-Christians happens elsewhere.

It's Relationships. Christ did not sacrifice Himself to establish an organization or a system of hierarchies. He did not die so that there would be grand buildings. He died so that we could be reconnected to the Community of the Godhead. He died so that we could have a relationship with Him, the Father and the Holy Spirit. He died so that we could be reconnected to the Source of Life. In doing so, Christ also gave us each other so that we would become part of His Holy Nation, we would be that spiritual Holy City, and we would be a part of His Community.

The Community of Christians has a distinct identity derived from Christ. The Community functions together as a single body. The members know each other intimately because they assemble frequently. Because of that knowledge the Community can act as one person, as one body, as one man.

17: PLAYING IN THE YARD

I have a secret pleasure. Since it's written here, it's not so much of a secret any more. The times when my family and friends get together and eat, talk, laugh, joke and play are the times most precious to me. Days like Thanksgiving, a feast day where relationships and thanks come first, are wonderful. What I like to do most is to sit back in the corner and listen and watch everyone being happy together. Happy. Joyful. Peaceful. Carefree. That is similar to the picture that was painted for us of Job's family as they all ate together: "His sons used to go and hold a feast in the house of each one on his day, and they would send and invite their three sisters to eat and drink with them." Job 1:4. God is the same way. He enjoys watching all His family work together and socialize together in peace and harmony. And being carefree all the while. He gives us things so we can enjoy them! 1 Timothy 6:17. These times are foretastes of the times when Jesus will "dine" with us and we with Him. Revelation 3:20.

Too many Christians look at life as a painful span of years of agony to be endured. Some people get this idea from Moses when he said, "As for the days of our life, they contain seventy years, Or if due to strength, eighty years, Yet their pride is *but* labor and sorrow; For soon it is gone and we fly away." Psalm 90. But that is really taken out of context. What is life like for a follower of God? Paul sums it up nicely: "But I say, walk by the Spirit, and you will not carry out the desire of the flesh... But if you are led by the Spirit, you are not under the Law... But the fruit of the Spirit is love, joy, peace, patience, kindness, goodness, faithfulness, gentleness, self-control; against such things there is no law. If we live by the Spirit, let us also walk by the Spirit." Galatians 5. So what do we have as Christians? We have love, joy, peace, patience, kindness, goodness, faithfulness, gentleness, self-control!

We also have that with our siblings in Christ in the Community. We have life abundantly. John 10:10. And there's more!

Rejoice! We should have a life of rejoicing. We have the Truth which was witnessed by Christ; therefore, we should "rejoice in truth." 1 Corinthians 13. The whole book of Philippians is a lesson on rejoicing! "What then? Only that in every way, whether in pretense or in truth, Christ is proclaimed; and in this I rejoice." "But even if I am being poured out as a drink offering upon the sacrifice and service of your faith, I rejoice and share my joy with you all. You too, I urge you, rejoice In the same way and share your joy with me." "Rejoice in the Lord always; again I will say, rejoice!" In Romans, Paul reminds us to "exult," which is rejoicing ratcheted up several notches: "...we exult in hope of the glory of God. And not only this, but we also exult in our tribulations." Romans 5. We should rejoice coming and going – whether we are up or down! But wait, there's still more!

Live like God. In His first recorded lesson to a large group, Jesus started by saying, "Blessed are the poor in spirit, for theirs is the kingdom of heaven." Jesus also said that "those who mourn," "the gentle," "those who hunger and thirst for righteousness," "the merciful," "the pure in heart," "the peacemakers," and "those who have been persecuted for the sake of righteousness" are all blessed. Some translate the word *blessed* as *happy*. But, that is not quite the meaning of *blessed* here. The word *blessed* is the Greek word *makarios*. It means more than just *blessed* or *happy*.

The meaning of *makarios* went through several changes in meaning over time. The first use was to refer to the life of the Greek gods. They were above all cares and free from labor and death. They lived in a world different and apart from mortals. To be "blessed" was to be a god. Then *makarios* came to refer to people who had died and were free from the cares of this life. Then the word went through one more change, *makarios* referred to the super wealthy of society. Their riches and power kept them from the problems of common people: they had no cares. In short, the super wealthy lived like the gods. They did not worry about where to live. They did not worry about food. They did not worry about what to wear. They lived free from fear and want. That is how God wants us to live. He wants us to participate in the same carefree, joyful life that the Father, the Son and the Holy Spirit experience.

Jesus wants us to live like God. He wants us to have the same blessed – *makarios* – existence that the Father, Son and Holy Spirit have. They need nothing, They have no cares. They have no fears. He tells us that we are "blessed" and that His followers have that same existence. Remember how Satan fills us with lies? Satan whispers in our ear that we don't have that *makarios* existence. Satan tells us we need to fear and worry. But, reality for Christians is just the opposite. In the "sermon on the mount," Jesus tells us we have that blessed life, that *makarios* life, now.

Jesus tells us not to worry about stashing up a big savings account. "Do not lay up for yourselves treasures on earth." Why not? Because we don't need to: God has everything covered. Jesus tells us not to be worried about what we are going to eat: He provides it. He tells us not to worry about clothes because He will make sure we are clothed. He said not to worry about our health or how long we will live: He has that covered, too. In fact, Jesus tells us He has everything covered that we need. In Mark 10, Jesus said, "Truly I say to you, there is no one who has left house or brothers or sisters or mother or father or children or farms, for My sake and for the gospel's sake, but that he will receive a hundred times as much now in the present age, houses and brothers and sisters and mothers and children and farms, along with persecutions; and in the age to come, eternal life." What do we have to worry about? If we believe God's promises – and God cannot lie – we should never have a worry or concern about anything physical!

Fear is a paralyzing emotion. It sets off the "fight or flight" response. Fear triggers anxiety. Anxiety creates mental and physical health issues. Fear kills. That is why Satan really wants us to doubt and fear. Think of the emotions and responses that are set off by fear! Fear causes anger, hatred, envy, jealousy, etc. If we go through the deeds of the flesh, we'll see that most of them are rooted in some type of fear: immorality, impurity, sensuality, idolatry, sorcery, enmities, strife, jealously, outbursts of anger, disputes, dissensions, factions, envying, drunkenness, and carousing. Galatians 5. Most of these things come from a primal, fleshly source: fear.

What is the opposite of fear? Love. Love bears that fruit of the Spirit. Love casts out fear and the negative emotions that we have and substitutes them with blessedness. John tells us, "There is no fear in love; but perfect love casts out fear, because fear involves punishment, and the one who fears is not perfected in love." 1 John 4. Since there is no condemnation for us, for those in Christ Jesus, we have no reason to be afraid of God.[38] Romans 8. In fact, in love we can call Him "Abba, Father," which is the English version of calling the Father "Daddy." Because we have no fear, we can approach His throne boldly. Hebrews 4:16 and Ephesians 2:12. Because we have been reconciled and are pure and blameless in his sight, we should feel as comfortable with God as we would with our closest friend. After all *He* has called us His friends.

Playing in the yard. Because we are at peace with God and are part of his family, what are we to be concerned about? Nothing. A friend says that we should feel like the children playing in the yard, while God, our Father, is sitting in the house writing the checks and paying the bills. When we live as God intends for us to live, we are fearless and carefree. Looking back at Adam and Eve in the Garden, they lived a similar life: no cares for any provisions for life and no fear of any kind. Christians can live spiritually in the Garden now. I believe that God enjoys watching his children all gather in peace, harmony and love much the way I enjoy my family and friends enjoying themselves.

All play and no work? Not quite. Confucious said, "Choose a job you love, and you will never have to work a day in your life." This is almost true. The work of a Christian is joyful. A wonderful description of the work of a follower of God is in Psalm 126: "Those who sow in tears shall reap with joyful shouting. He who goes to and fro weeping, carrying his bag of seed, Shall indeed come again with a shout of joy, bringing his sheaves with him." Jesus referred to this Psalm in John 4, when He said, "Already he who reaps is receiving wages and is gathering fruit for life eternal; so that he who sows and he who reaps may rejoice together. For in this *case* the saying is true, 'One sows and another reaps.' I sent you to reap that for which you have not labored; others have labored and you have entered into their labor." We all share in the work. The work may be hard at times, but there is always joy at the end. The sower and reaper can "rejoice together."

How difficult is this labor? Jesus said, "Come to Me, all who are weary and heavy-laden, and I will give you rest. Take My yoke upon you and learn from Me, for I am gentle and humble in heart, and you will find rest for your souls. For My yoke is easy and My burden is light." Matthew 11. Why is our work

---

[38] I am not saying we should not revere God. We should not be afraid or terrified of Him.

"light"? It's not heavy or burdensome because our work for God should come naturally. It should come to us as naturally as play is to a child. It's just what Christians do. We enjoy serving others. We love to praise God. We are so ecstatic about what God has done for us, we can't help but share. David said that working for God delighted him:

I delight to do Your will, O my God;

Your Law is within my heart."

I have proclaimed glad tidings of righteousness in the great congregation;

Behold, I will not restrain my lips,

O Lord, You know.

I have not hidden Your righteousness within my heart;

I have spoken of Your faithfulness and Your salvation;

I have not concealed Your lovingkindness and Your truth from the great congregation.

Psalm 40. As joyful Christians we "Proclaim good tidings of His salvation from day to day." Both men and women proclaim the gospel: "the women who proclaim the good tidings are a great host..." Psalms 96 and 68.

Even when things get rough, these are causes for celebration. "We exult in our tribulation!" Romans 5. When Peter and John were brought before the Jewish leaders after a lame man was healed and the leaders chastised them, they and the other Christians praised God and sang Psalms. Acts 4. Then, when the Apostles were flogged after healing others, they rejoiced. "So they went on their way from the presence of the Council, rejoicing that they had been considered worthy to suffer shame for His name." Acts 5. Paul said our afflictions are light when compared with the weight of our eternal glory: when afflictions come they are a reason for us to rejoice! 2 Corinthians 4:17 and 7:4.

Christ cheerfully loved, served, encouraged and taught all people. He did so because that was His nature. His actions arose from His very being. As the sun shines just because that's what it is, so Jesus shines because that is who He is. As Christians, we have taken on the mind of Christ. 1 Corinthians 2:16. Love, service, encouragement, praise and teaching are just part of who we are. It's what we like to do. It makes us happy. It's just who we are!

As followers of Christ, we *get* to do the things for God just because we love to do them. We do these things because of who we are. Our service for

God should feel like play, something that we look forward to in the morning and something that we are disappointed in when we have to stop at night. Doing the things of God should be as natural to a Christian as flight and song are to a bird.

We can do all of these things in a carefree way, because we are God's children out in the yard "playing" while the Father is in the house making sure we have everything we need.

As part of a Community, Christians are carefree and joyful. Even when we are persecuted for Christ, we rejoice. Because we have the mind of Christ, our "work" for God is joyful. It is an outward expression of our inward being. We just do what comes naturally from our newly minted Christian hearts, while we allow God to supply all the resources.

18: ASSEMBLING A COMMUNITY

Along roadsides, wildflowers sometimes almost seem to appear in puddles of bright colors. Usually they are all one species and one color that grow in a patch. Some patches are large, like Texas bluebonnets in the spring. Others are small little colonies. There is a reason they clump together: a seed of that particular variety was somehow planted there, produced more seed and, therefore, more flowers. Wind, birds, or highway mowers spread the seed to another site where a new little colony of flowers started up on its own. These bouquets of flowers happen naturally, organically, by God's own plan.

Bloom where you're planted. Forming a Community is not a hard thing to do. Since you're a Christian, the hard work has been done for you – fellow Christians are probably all around you. If you are a member of a Church, you can pull together a group of fellow believers to form a tightly knit Community, who are willing to edify each other, take on the burdens of others, and to be "naked" (confessing and not hiding your sins and struggles). It can be a mix of however many people you feel comfortable with. Some have found that about 8 to 12 Christians is a good number. You may find that your entire congregation is your Community. You may face rejection because of the reality that many and perhaps most will never be able to get "spiritually naked" – reveal fears, doubts, troubles, struggles, and sins – because the idea is the complete antithesis of Church. Remember, the ekklesia, the Community, is a place where there is no judgment. On one occasion in a Community, one member expressed a doubt about something most Christians take for granted. A visitor to that Community almost came unglued: "A Christian can't doubt _____!" Christians can and will have doubts about many things. Doubting and resolving doubts are how we grow spiritually. This group also learned that the presence of visitors who don't understand how God's Communities work are not always a good idea.

On the other hand, the constraints may be how many people can fit into a house or a room. Remember the 5000 Christians in Jerusalem? They were all one, but they met in small Communities from house to house daily. If that large number did occasionally assemble together, they probably met in the same way Jesus taught in large numbers, in open areas outdoors outside cities. I have been told that some mega-Churches function as a large Community of Communities. Instead of being a Church/Community of 2000 people, in reality they function as a Community of 100 Communities. A Community is not an exclusive group; it is an inclusive group. Follow Christ's example. Include. Don't exclude. Varying age groups and experiences will only bring richness to your Community. But there is a better way.

A note of caution. Thinking of the ekklesia as a Community rather than as a Church, an institution, may be too radical an idea or change for the leaders in your Church. The leadership of your Church may not understand what an ekklesia, a Community, really is. They may try to preserve the institution. These leaders are acting from their faith and their best understanding. Nevertheless, the leaders may feel that they are losing control when small communities meet. The leaders may have a misperception that their roles are to act as gatekeepers and censors and may unintentionally stifle individual growth. Do not rebel against your leaders. Both Christ and Paul showed respect to the sinful, murderous High Priests when they were being persecuted. Leaders who are trying to do their best should not be given less respect. Leaders of Churches who do not condone Christians meeting in Communities should be heeded. This leaves you a choice: either stay where you are and submit, or you leave that Church. If you decide to leave, do so in peace and quietly and without a spirit of rebellion. If you decide to remain, stay peacefully and without remorse or grudge.

Starting an *ekklesia*. Starting a Community. Not every Christian will jump at the chance to be part of a Community. As strange as it sounds, many people are converted to a religion or to a Church and not to Christ. Inertia also has a big factor from keeping people trying something "different." Fear of the unknown or unfamiliar will keep some from tasting of the full relationship with a Community of God's people. So don't be surprised that devout persons do not readily jump into a Community.

Find individual Christians who are seeking. They don't necessarily need to be from your "Church." Then meet together. Meet whenever you can. Use texts and email to encourage and to ask for help. One group met early in the morning. Some women met in the mid afternoon. You can meet in a house or apartment. You can meet in a park. You can meet in a building, an office, a library. You have everything you need. You have the scriptures. You have each other. You have the Spirit of God. Romans 8. You have Christ. Matthew 18:20.

A Community does not mean rejection of authority. Many people have the mistaken idea that Communities of believers meeting in homes or nontraditional locations means they are trying to evade the authority of Elders or Overseers. Think of the way cities and tribes operated in Israel. Each Community had its own elders who oversaw the city, the Community. It should be the same way in God's Communities. When a Community is grounded enough to have mature men qualified to act as Elders or Overseers, that Community needs to be led by them. A Community with leaders will be more active and dynamic. It will function as God meant for His Community to function.

Your Church can become one of God's Communities. It is possible for a Church to function as a Community. That is actually the ideal situation. However, it will take a very big shift in thinking – an almost seismic shift. If your Church has a professional Preacher, his work will change and will be focused outside: he should be willing to become an apostle of the Community. This may mean at various times he leaves the location where the Community assembles. The direction of the Community comes from the Elders, Pastors, or Shepherds. They will be leaders and orchestrators. As with a flock, the shepherds will walk ahead without coercing the flock to follow. They will need to be patient men who can and will get to know each member of the flock personally. They need to be like Christ, willing to give their lives for their charges. Teaching and care becomes these Elders' primary functions. This may mean that a person who is a leader in a Church steps down if he cannot teach. 1 Timothy 3:2. This is not an institution to be operated through surrogates, subordinates or deputies: the Community must have leaders who lead and teach personally.

The focus. The individual members will need to act like a Community instead of a Church. Rather than being a passive audience, each member should contribute at each assembly. This also means that you will want to change the way you sit. Rather than look forward at a platform or pulpit, the focus of the assembly is God and each other. Looking at the person on the other side of the room becomes part of what you do and is not a distraction from what you are doing. Focusing on those around you is what you are there for. For example, if a man is sleepy and nodding off, he shouldn't be chastised: we should find out what is wrong with him and help him out. He might be sick, working too hard, or have some other problem the Community can help with. When someone is tearful, we stop and take time to support and care for her. If someone is particularly withdrawn, the Community will find out why and look to support him. It may happen that the entire meeting of the Community becomes helping a single member. When one of the members of the Community is missing, his or her absence is palpable: it is felt by all.

Communing. When we take of the Lord's Supper, we see and speak and sing to each other. It becomes a sharing experience, a communal or Community event. "Is not the cup of blessing which we bless a sharing in the blood of Christ? Is not the bread which we break a sharing in the body of Christ? Since there is one bread, we who are many are one body; for we all partake of the one bread." 1 Corinthians 10. I can see the tear in my sister's eye when we talk of Christ's suffering. I can see the joy in all of our faces when we talk of His resurrection. The Lord's Supper in reality becomes a Communion of the Community. (See the King James and New King James translation of 1 Corinthians 10:16.) We do not just commune with God, we commune with each other. We are priests sharing in the sacrifice! Communion reinforces our oneness.

Singing. When the members of the Community sing, they sing to each other. They speak to one another. Ephesians 5:19. They sing songs that have meaning to them and give instruction and comfort. "Each one has a psalm." 1 Corinthians 14. It may be that a particular hymn has meaning or has been placed on their heart: the Spirit is not quenched. 1 Thessalonians 5. His presence is vital to the Community. So what some people see as a music ministry will not be a part of the Community. Because "each one has a Psalm," a song leader or music minister is unnecessary. Familiar songs may start to be sung spontaneously. We will not sing things we don't understand: "I will sing [psalms] with the Spirit and I will sing [psalms] with the mind also." 1 Corinthians 14. We may stop after singing a psalm and use it as a basis for deeper understanding of God.

Reading. Teaching. How would you like to be taught by Christ Himself? You can. Read the Gospels. How would you like to be taught by the men Jesus selected to be His witnesses and messengers? You can. Read what the Apostles wrote. "So then, brethren, stand firm and hold to the traditions which you were taught, whether by word of mouth or by letter from us." 2 Thessalonians 2. Paul wrote something very interesting to Timothy:

Until I come, give attention to the public reading of Scripture, to exhortation and teaching... Take pains with these things; be absorbed in them, so that your progress will be evident to all. Pay close attention to yourself and to your teaching; persevere in these things, for as you do this you will ensure salvation both for yourself and for those who hear you.

1 Timothy 4. Paul wanted Timothy "to be absorbed" in reading, exhortation and teaching. What was Timothy supposed to read? What was he to be absorbed in? Peter tells us:

...[J]ust as also our beloved brother Paul, according to the wisdom given him, wrote to you, as also in all his letters, speaking in them of these things, in which are some things hard to understand, which the untaught and unstable distort, as they do also the rest of the Scriptures, to their own destruction.

2 Peter 3:16. Peter said that Paul's writings were part of the Scriptures. Paul intended his letters to be shared among Christians in different cities: Colossians 4:16 and 1 Thessalonians 5:27. Historically, we know that the early Christians concentrated on reading the writings of the Apostles. Polycarp, who was taught by the Apostle John, wrote:

[Paul], when among you, accurately and steadfastly taught the word of truth in the presence of those who were then alive. And when absent from you, he wrote you letters, which if you carefully study, you will find to be the means of building you up in that faith which has been given you, and which, being followed by hope, and preceded by love towards God, and Christ, and our neighbor, "is the mother of us all."

Polycarp, Chapter 3.

What are Paul's letters and the letters of the other Apostles? They are instructions and teachings for individual Communities of Christians. Who are we? We are individual Communities of Christians. The letters were written and meant to be shared: "When this letter is read among you, have it also read in the church of the Laodiceans; and you, for your part read my letter that is coming from Laodicea."[39] Colossians 4. Although we are separated by continents and centuries, the letters were meant to be shared among all Communities of Christians throughout the world and throughout time.

How does this teaching happen? First, let the authorities speak. Read the Scriptures to the Community. The original recipients were Communities facing similar problems and challenges to those that your Community faces or may face. Second, follow the example of the Community in Nehemiah 8: they heard the scriptures read, and then they discussed them in small groups so that the meaning was clear. This is apparently the way of teaching that Paul had in mind when he wrote to Timothy. Teaching this way leaves the biggest burden of teaching to the Apostles, the witnesses and messengers, sent by God to teach us. This way of teaching also avoids jumping from "proof text" to "proof text" which too often are easily distorted by the "untaught and unstable."

Getting naked. Not literally. As we become comfortable with our fellow members, we should not have shame (a fear-driven emotion) over our sins and shortcomings. We all have sinned. If Paul could freely admit that he was "the chief of sinners," being responsible for the deaths of many of his fellow Christians, should we have any less difficulty sharing our weaknesses? Secrets only have power over us as long as we keep them secret. When known, sin makes living a double life more difficult if not impossible. Once they are known, others with similar struggles can help us and we can help them.

Did you know that 34% of churchgoing women have visited pornography sites? It has been found that 50% of men in Church on Sunday morning visited a pornographic site the week before. Even more startling is that 54% of the pastors and preachers watch pornography weekly. I have a Christian friend who was a porn addict – he couldn't stop. He went to a Christian counselor for help. His counselor's advice? Confess: tell his son that he was

---

[39] The letter coming from Laodicea was probably the Letter to the Ephesians because Laodicea is between the two cities, and Paul's Ephesian letter would have been delivered to Ephesus, then through Laodicea, and finally to Collosae.

addicted to pornography. Suddenly, the cravings subsided or were easier to handle. The son found new respect for his father because he was willing to "be naked" about his shortcomings. Because he has admitted them, he has overcome his addiction.

According to statistics, almost 3.5% of the population describe themselves as homosexual or bisexual. The Kinsey Report put the number as high as 10 percent. If you have a Church of 100 people, three or four people (or possibly as many as ten) are battling homosexual desires or are engaging is homosexual acts. Most of them are secretly battling their desires in shame and fear. In a Community they can confess their secret struggles openly without condemnation: they find support and understanding and avoid feeling and fighting alone. In Churches, a Christian can't confess these things: he or she would be labeled a "bad Christian" because it is thought that "real Christians" don't have such struggles. All Christians have struggles: a "gay" Christian just has different ones.

With all this in mind, the Community realizes that it is the individual, ultimately, that heals himself. Although the Community may want to solve the other Christian's problems, only the individual can make changes to his soul with the aid of the Holy Spirit. We must avoid creating codependency relationships within the Community.[40] Much of the time, the Community may do nothing but listen. We will be the crowd on the sidelines cheering the struggling Christian toward godliness. Remember, sports teams tend to win more frequently when they are on their home fields with their own fans cheering them on. In a Community, every Christian is a "fan" of every other Christian.

Christians are not alone. These are several examples of sins and temptations. Many other weaknesses inflict every Christian. Too often, we try to "go it alone" or be strong individually. When we "go it alone," we will fail. Guaranteed. What great comfort and assurance it is that when we open up, we have the love and support of all the other members of the Community. So that my weakness is aided by your strength; your weakness could be aided by another yet believer. Paul explained how this works:

---

[40] A codependency relationship is one in which the Community takes on the responsibility for solving the problems of a person. Because the codependent persons haven't taken responsibility for working on his own problem, he gets no closer to a solution. Usually the Community actually impedes a solution or aggravates the problem.

Now we who are strong ought to bear the weaknesses of those without strength and not just please ourselves. Each of us is to please his neighbor for his good, to his edification. For even Christ did not please Himself; but as it is written, "The reproaches of those who reproached You fell on Me." For whatever was written in earlier times was written for our instruction, so that through perseverance and the encouragement of the Scriptures we might have hope. Now may the God who gives perseverance and encouragement grant you to be of the same mind with one another according to Christ Jesus, so that with one accord you may with one voice glorify the God and Father of our Lord Jesus Christ. Therefore, accept one another, just as Christ also accepted us to the glory of God.

Romans 15. As Christians, our sins are covered by the blood of Christ. God sees them no longer. The greater the sin we have means that the grace and mercy poured out on us is greater still. Our forgiveness is a greater cause for us to love Him all the more. "For this reason I say to you, her sins, which are many, have been forgiven, for she loved much; but he who is forgiven little, loves little." Luke 7. Ultimately, Christians confess their sins, shortcomings and trials freely to each other in their Community of believers. Rather than seeing the sin, the Community will see the magnificence of God's love, mercy and grace. The Community will see its role in lovingly helping the struggling member. The Community will praise God for His boundless mercy and love.

Saying nothing. Unconfessed, our weaknesses become our downfall. Unconfessed, our pride and trusting in our own strength obscures God's greatness. It is only when we are weak that God's strength shows through. As God told Paul, "My grace is sufficient for you, for power is perfected in weakness." 2 Corinthians 12. When David confessed his sin with Bathsheba and the murder of her husband, relief and praise and spreading the good news of God's mercy and grace were the result:

Be gracious to me, O God, according to Your lovingkindness;
According to the greatness of Your compassion blot out my transgressions.
Wash me thoroughly from my iniquity
And cleanse me from my sin.
...Behold, You desire truth in the innermost being,

And in the hidden part You will make me know wisdom.

...Create in me a clean heart, O God,

And renew a steadfast spirit within me.

...Restore to me the joy of Your salvation

And sustain me with a willing spirit.

Then I will teach transgressors Your ways,

And sinners will be converted to You.

Deliver me from bloodguiltiness, O God, the God of my salvation;

Then my tongue will joyfully sing of Your righteousness.

O Lord, open my lips,

That my mouth may declare Your praise.

Psalm 51. Living a life with no hidden sins creates an out pouring of praise and a spreading of the good news to all. "Let him who boasts, boast in the Lord." 1 Corinthians 1. We boast in God because He delights in grace, justice and righteousness. "Let not a wise man boast of his wisdom, and let not the mighty man boast of his might, let not a rich man boast of his riches; but let him who boasts boast of this, that he understands and knows Me, that I am the Lord who exercises lovingkindness [grace], justice and righteousness on earth; for I delight in these things." Jeremiah 9.

When all members of the Community, even the shepherds, live without false pretenses, the Community strengthens and grows. This also gives those outside of Christ a true picture of who they can be: forgiven sinners, glorified beings, and adopted children of God. Keeping mum deprives God of communal praise and our heartfelt gratitude. Silence about our shortcomings often makes Christians rightly appear to be hypocrites.

What do we do? If we start a Community, what will we do? I don't know what your Community will do. If you have come from a Church, you will probably expect to be told what to do and when. You might expect an "order of services" designed locally, by tradition or by the denomination. In a Community, no single person sets out the order of "services." Most of what Christians consider part of a "worship service" are actually things that Christians should be doing throughout the week anyway. I can almost guarantee that you won't start "on time." You will probably "wait one for another." 1 Corinthians 11. As people gather, they will catch up on what's happening in each other's lives and struggles they are going through. An impromptu song may start the group to praise God. Someone may confess a weakness or a need to be built up in faith: the Community may stop right then and there to pray. Another person may read a scripture that helped him through the week. You will not hear a sermon, per se. A point of faith might take up the full time as people share struggles. The elders of the Community will gently guide their flock into deeper understandings. Eventually a member of the Community may say something about Christ's death and resurrection, which may then lead into the Lord's Supper if the gathering is on a Sunday. And it won't necessarily be taken at the same time in the gathering. Expect the group to converse about the Lord's Supper or sing about it before, after, and maybe during the time the Community is communing. Or you may not sing at all!. I have attended gatherings where the whole focus was an unplanned discussion of the crucifixion and resurrection. The Community may plan a work or project to do together, such as feeding the hungry or housing the homeless: you will reach out to serve others as Christ did. Don't be surprised if the Community wants to stay together to share a meal. Don't be surprised if the Community wants to linger together for hours more. Don't be surprised if you can't get enough togetherness.

What should you expect? Prayer, praise, encouragement, enlightenment, communing, unburdening of sin and guilt, and humble service. Expect the Holy Spirit to work in you and each other person of the Community. Expect the Holy Spirit to be the unifying force in your gathering. Ephesians 4. If you are sensitive to Him, your movement and growth may appear baffling and mysterious to others as things just happen for you and doors and opportunities are opened to you just when you need them to be. "The wind blows where it wishes and you hear the sound of it, but do not know where it comes from and where it is going; so is everyone who is born of the Spirit." John 3. Let the Master Renovator step into your Community and be prepared to be amazed. I have witnessed a person read a scripture that was important to her that day: then a discussion ensued that was precisely what strengthened another Christian in the Community who sheltered a secret doubt or struggle. If you join or start a Community, your life will be changed forever. If you are like most Christians participating in a Community, you will grow more spiritually than you ever dreamed was possible. One woman said she grew more in one year in a Community than she had in fifty years of "going to Church."

Ideally. In an ideal situation, you would exchange your institutional Church experience for a Community experience. Your Community, your *ekklesia*, should become your primary connection to the Godhead and to other Christians. Although there may be some value in starting a Community while you are still a member of a Church, your full potential is not there. When you replace Church with a Community as your main connection to God and your fellow saints and make the Community your main group for worship and encouragement, you will understand the richness of God's plan and experience a taste of heaven in this lifetime. The Community may form smaller groups to work intently on one member's weakness. However you do it, it will whet your appetite for more spiritual things and an aching longing to be with Christ. "As deer for streams, I pant for God." You will find that you, too, will grow, and wax strong in spirit, will be filled with wisdom: and the grace of God will be upon you. Luke 2:40.

A Community can be started anywhere by anyone. A Community is a safe place for love and forgiveness. The Community freely confesses their shortcomings to each other and the Community does not judge them but encourages and strengthens them. The elders of the Community teach from the scriptures. A Community gathers frequently, almost daily. The focus of all the gatherings of the Community is God and the other members of the Community. It is lead by the Holy Spirit.

19: A BODY AT REST

To say that Isaac Newton was a brilliant man is an understatement. He discovered mathematical principles of motion that scientists and astronomers still use today, even though he wrote them about 350 years ago. His first law of motion is, simply stated, an object either is at rest or moves at a constant velocity, unless acted upon by an external force. Or, as viewed another way, an object that is sitting still won't move unless something moves it. It is the law of inertia.

Our human bodies were never meant to "be at rest." Sedentary jobs (work where one rarely leaves a chair or does any strenuous activity) may be the cause of many diseases and may contribute to the early deaths of many people. Some studies connect the rise in obesity rates in the United States to the rise in the number of sedentary jobs. Heart problems, diabetes and other diseases can be directly linked to our lack of physical activity. Our bodies were made for work and movement. As a spiritual body, we were also made for work and movement. However, with many groups, they are weighed down by inertia and tend to "stay at rest." It takes effort to get out of a pew. Therefore spiritual illnesses abound. "For this reason many among you are weak and sick, and a number sleep." 1 Corinthians 11.

Communities at rest. Rest is essential for a body. Rest is essential for a Community, too. Rest is one of the underlying principles of work and creation. However, as God demonstrated, rest comes after work and before work. Unfortunately, many Communities of God's people are weighed down by inertia. They are at rest. Because they have been "saved," what more do they need to do? They do not break the inertia of being at rest, being satisfied with "one anothering." As a sedentary body, the Community tends to do less and less. A Community tends to turn inward, ignoring the outside world. A resting Community will become self-righteous and self-satisfied. In short, the Community constantly at rest will risk becoming a Church.

Turning outward. A paradox exists in the life of a Christian. The life of a Christian consists in *being* and not *doing*. Some theologians, pastors and preachers have taken this to an extreme, extolling that because there is nothing you can do to merit salvation, then there is nothing for you to do after you've become a Christian. As a result, Christians bask under the UV lamps of faith-only or grace-only thinking they are in contact with the real source of Light. On the other hand, if we do things only because of a "duty to God," we are "unworthy slaves; we have done *only* that which we ought to have done." Luke 17:10. Being saved by grace and faith doesn't mean we give up on serving him. Paul told Titus, that our good deeds grow from our God's grace and mercy:

> He saved us, not on the basis of deeds which we have done in righteousness, but according to His mercy, by the washing of regeneration and renewing by the Holy Spirit, whom He poured out upon us richly through Jesus Christ our Savior, so that being justified by His grace we would be made heirs according to *the* hope of eternal life. This is a trustworthy statement; and concerning these things I want you to speak confidently, so that those who have believed God will be careful to engage in good deeds. These things are good and profitable for men.

Titus 3:5-8. Notice that the "good deeds" arise after we are washed and renewed. They are not something we do to *earn* salvation. They are things we do *because* we are already saved. As we are renovated into the image of Christ through the working of the Holy Spirit, our "good deeds" will merely be a reflection of who we are just as God's good deeds are a reflection of His divine nature.

Creeds and Codes. Man-made codes do not protect us spiritually. As Paul said, they have the *appearance* of wisdom, but are of no value against fleshly indulgence. Colossians 2:20-23. Some groups try to reduce the gospel to a written list of creeds, beliefs, do's, don't's, etc. There is no checklist of things that we can do and can't do. There is no list of good deeds that we need to do. There is no percentage of what we have that we have to give. There is no set number of volunteer hours or community service for Christians. Every talent, every resource and every breath is a gift from God; therefore, how much of our lives should we give to Him?

Although we are dead to the "elemental spiritual forces of this world", we must pay attention to people who are in the world. Colossians 2:20. "Pure and undefiled religion in the sight of *our* God and Father is this: to visit orphans and widows in their distress, *and* to keep oneself unstained by the world." James 1:27. Or, as James said later, "Faith without works is dead." James 2:26. Faith requires action.

Being means Doing. Why does a seed grow into a plant? The seed contains at its core, in its DNA, all the instructions for making a plant. Surrounding this core are nutrients sufficient to get the seed started growing until it can start making its own food from sunlight. When the right amounts of water and warmth are present, the seed germinates and becomes a plant. Then that plant produces fruit and more seeds. A seed grows into a plant because *that is what it is.*

Have you ever wondered why the Sun shines or the stars sparkle? When gases collect in space, the individual atoms are attracted to each other and eventually create a strong point of gravity to attract more gases, which in turn pulls in more gases and material from space until it becomes tightly compacted. When all these elements become compacted, they "ignite" – so to speak – and a chain reaction starts the ball of gas to shine. Why does it shine? It shines because *that's what it is.*

So, what about Christians? Throughout the New Testament, we read about Christians sharing, giving and doing. In Acts 2 we read that they had "all things in common." Barnabas sold some of his property and gave the proceeds to help other believers. We know of the sacrificial service they gave to one another and to the world. But why? Christians did not give or serve under compulsion. Philemon 1 and 2 Corinthians 9. They were not coerced by guilt to tithe a certain percentage. Christians do these things cheerfully because it is *who we are.* Praise and good deeds are our cheerful sacrifices to God. Hebrews 13.

As God does good things for us because of who He is, we should do good things because of who we are – creatures being made into the image of God, the first fruits of creation. James 2. If we do good things solely out of a sense of "duty to God," we are "unworthy slaves; we have done only that which we ought to have done." Luke 17. Rather, our good deeds emanate from our very being. We love and bless our enemies. We give without ever thinking about being repaid. We impoverish ourselves for the sake of others. We can freely give because we are not giving just of ourselves: we are giving what God has blessed us with. We pass God's blessings on to others. As Christians, all that we are and have belong to God. We are instruments in passing on to others what God has given us. A full pitcher cannot be refilled unless it is emptied. As we pass on the blessings that have been given to us, we then have more space for even more blessings. Our bowl of flour and jar of oil will always be full no matter how often we empty them. (Remember the widow at Zarephath. 1 Kings 17.) God will bless us with necessities as we give to others what He has given us. Philippians 4.

Collectively, we should shine like the sun. As each Christian is attracted to another Christian and then to another Christian after that, we collectively ignite the love and light that each of us has individually, and form a more massive instrument for good than we could not do alone. As a united Community serving others selflessly with God on our side, nothing we purpose to do will be impossible for us. Genesis 11. What is impossible for one person to do, a Community can do easily. If we lack a particular skill, talent or resource, the Holy Spirit will supply whatever we are lacking to accomplish his service. Ephesians 4.

Relationships with Purpose. Many people see service to others as an end in and of itself. There is great value in expressing God's love for other people through our selfless acts. However, caring for others' physical needs doesn't feed their souls. As Christians, we need to look deeper. Many prayer requests are for non-Christian family members or coworkers to be physically healed: For what purpose? So they may go on sinning and being alienated from God? Rather, we should pray foremost and fervently that they will come to know Jesus Christ. Feeding, clothing and housing people only takes care of physical needs for a short time. What people really need is to be spiritually fed by Christ, clothed in spotless robes by God, and to become a dwelling for the Holy Spirit.

Caring for others should not be superficial. God does not care for us out of a sense of duty or obligation: His care is an expression of His love. It is an expression of His being. When we help house the homeless or provide meals for the hungry, we are expressing God's love for all humanity. In Psalm 72 Solomon says, "For he [Christ] will deliver the needy when he cries for help, The afflicted also, and him who has no helper. He will have compassion on the poor and needy, And the lives of the needy he will save. He will rescue their life from oppression and violence, And their blood will be precious in his sight...." In this life we are tools of Christ, His body in this world. We literally act on his behalf. As Christ will say to us, "Truly I say to you, to the extent that you did it to one of these brothers of Mine, even the least of them, you did it to Me." Matthew 25. Our care for others grows out of Christ's love flowing through us and from His genuine love for our fellow human beings, which has become our love, too. As with Christ, our actions arise from love and not guilt.

While we express our genuine love for others by caring for their physical needs, the people of the world will also learn of our love for them as spiritual beings, too. When people realize our pure motives for their well-being – not only for things physical but also for things spiritual – they will be more open to and accepting of the Good News of Christ's love for them, too. Without love for others, we are nothing more than a bunch of ATMs dispensing food, clothes and money. "If I give all my possessions to feed the poor... but do not have love, it profits me nothing." 1 Corinthinans 13. Our care should primarily be for souls; however, we also care for the earthen vessels containing those souls. 2 Corinthians 4:7.

Draft Dodging. During the American civil war, a wealthy man could pay to have a poor man go to battle for him. The Conscription Act of 1863 allowed men to avoid the draft by paying $300. The poor couldn't afford to pay, so they fought and died. We cannot pay our way out of serving God. But in practice, many people act as though they have a paid surrogate working in their place on the battlefield.

Some people don't visit the ailing in hospitals or take care of the spiritually weak. Many do not teach others about God's love. Sadly, too, many don't study the scriptures. Why? Because they think they've paid someone to do it for them. That's the preacher's job. That's what he gets paid for. Hospitals even acknowledge this tradition by reserving special "clergy" parking spaces. Why should I study the bible when I'm paying someone to study it for me and give me lessons two or three times a week? Why dig into the feast of the scriptures when predigested lessons in a workbook? A sermon or Bible lesson is not a substitute for studying and learning for yourself. We are satisfied with a frozen, microwave meal when we should be hungering for the banquet God has set out for us in the presence of our enemies. Psalm 23.

Caring for others – both physically and spiritually – is a non-delegable duty.[41] A "non-delegable duty" is a responsibility we can't hand off to someone else or to pay another to do for us. We cannot get someone to do our job for us. For example, in American legal terms, the maintenance of the brakes on your car is a non-delegable duty: it is *your* job to make sure your brakes work. If they fail, it is your fault that they failed even though you just paid $200 to have them repaired. In the same way, you can't pay your way out of doing what you are supposed to do. Expressing the love you have for others is something that only you can do.

In orphanages, babies die because they are not loved. They have the physical necessities of life, but they lack the emotional necessities of life. Of those who survive infancy, most suffer from mental illness for the rest of their lives.[42] Why do we think that adults are any less complicated? A homeless woman expressed her sense of being unloved one frigid night when people rescued stray dogs from the cold but left homeless men and women to the freezing elements. It is not the distribution of food, clothes or blankets that heals a soul: it is the love of Christ being lavished on the unloved. The expression of love can only happen when one individual touches another individual's life personally. When one not only touches a life, but latches onto it as though it was their life, too. As Christ said, "A new commandment I give to you, that you love one another, even as I have loved you, that you also love one another." John 13. "Truly I say to you, to the extent that you did it to one of these brothers of Mine, *even* the least *of them*, you did it to Me." Matthew 25:40. Jesus says that we are to love our fellow human-beings as He loved us: with our very existence. It may be easy to die for a righteous man; but would you be willing to give a few bucks to an unrighteous beggar? Christ gave His life for us while we were poor, unrighteous beggars: so destitute that we were ashamed even to look up to beg, which is the description of our poverty in Matthew 5. Why should we do less for others? As Jesus said, "Give to him who asks of you, and do not

[41] If your brakes were to fail, you are responsible for their failure. You may have a legal action against the maintenance shop. But, the responsibility to make sure they work is on you, and you alone!

[42] http://www.huffingtonpost.com/maia-szalavitz/how-orphanages-kill-babie_b_549608.html, retrieved October 4, 2013.

turn away from him who wants to borrow from you." Matthew 5:42. If we die while serving God, what is that to us? Romans 14:8.

Christ's body, the *ekklesia*, was made to work. As certainly as we are saved by faith and grace, by faith and grace we work for others. Christ died for us while we were His enemies: shouldn't we be willing to do as much or more as long as we live?

AFTERWARD

Let's get back to the title of this book, *The Church does not Exist*. Does it indeed exist? Definitely not in the way that most people believe it does. The primary idea behind Christ's *ekklesia* is relationships: relationships with the Father, the Son and the Holy Spirit and then relationships with fellow Christians. God's path is marked with cairns and signposts that lead us into relationships with God and our fellow Christians. Therefore, *Church* is a pretty lousy word to describe these relationships, much less any relationship. The way Church functions in most places throughout the world is contrary to what the Father planned, what Christ died for, and what the Holy Spirit is building.

God had planned from the foundation of creation for a new species of spiritual creature to be brought into fellowship with the Godhead. The "first fruits among His creatures." He planned to create a special group of spiritual beings, a new creation (Galatians 6:15) that are to be part of a Community with Him: special spiritual creatures that commune with Him. As Christ said, "Behold, I stand at the door and knock; if anyone hears My voice and opens the door, I will come in to him and will dine with him, and he with Me." Revelation 3:20. Christ is not saying that if we allow Him in that He'll take us out to dinner. He is saying that we will have the close, personal relationship with Him – like friends who casually share dinner with each other and enjoy each other's company. The King James version says that we "commune" with Him and with other believers. 1 Corinthians 10. It staggers the imagination the God wants to be with me. God wants me to know Him as well as He knows me. 1 Corinthians 13:12. God wants to be a loving, generous Father to me. God wants me to be His friend. God wants me to have the most intimate of relations with Him, as member of the Bride of Jesus Christ. The single fact that He wants any of those relationships with me leaves me stupefied.

As Christians, we are a nation, a people, a family, a priesthood, and branches of the vine. In short, we are a Community. Specifically, we are God's Community. We are the *ekklesia*. As members of the Community, we have relationships that are not mere acquaintances. We have relationships that are founded on the deepest bedrock that exists and that are reinforced daily, and endure through eternity.

Some readers of this book may think I have "a morbid interest in controversial questions and disputes about words." However, nothing in the book arises from "envy, strife, abusive language, evil suspicions, and constant friction between men of depraved mind and deprived of the truth, who suppose that godliness is a means of gain." 1 Timothy 6. I am praying for godliness to increase among Christians. Words have meanings. Sometimes a foreign word does not have an exact translation in English. Still other times, religious constraints and personal beliefs of the translators cloud over obvious meanings and an inferior word usurps its place. The word *ekklesia* is a victim of translation. The word *church,* an inherently religious word, has eclipsed the elegant idea of *community.*

For those who have read this book and still do not agree with my conclusions, peace. From the outset, I knew that many – maybe even most – readers would not agree with my current understandings. You may still consider the Church to be an organization and that the institution, rules, and other appurtenances are necessary or desirable. You may never be comfortable with the idea of God's people being a Community. However, I hope that you will have patience and compassion for those who are seeking a deeper relationship with God and with fellow believers through means other that the institution of "Church." Please don't condemn those who meet together in small groups to work collectively for mutual edification and praise. Please open your minds to consider that there may be different ways to assemble that do not involve a building, a preacher and a formal order. Christians can have richly blessed lives that do not involve many of the trappings that are usually found in traditional Churches.

The same warning is for those who are in Communities rather than traditional Churches. Church members are your siblings, your fellow citizens, and God's chosen people. They are doing things differently. Do not judge. You can strengthen and encourage each other often. You can learn from people in traditional Churches and that they can learn from you.

Above all, seek for God's glory, God's unity and God's love so that Christ's pleas to the Father will be realized: "The glory which You have given Me I have given to them, that they may be one, just as We are one; I in them and You in Me, that they may be perfected in unity, so that the world may know that You sent Me, and loved them, even as You have loved Me." John 17:22-23.

Grace, mercy and peace to you from God our Father, the Lord Jesus Christ our Savior, and the Holy Spirit dwelling within you.

Tom Mann

SELECTED BIBLIOGRAPHY

Bercot, David W. *Will the Real Heretics Please Stand Up: A New Look at Today's Evangelical Church in the Light of Early Christianity.* Henderson, TX: Scroll Pub., 1989. Print.

Cloud, Henry, and John Sims Townsend. *How People Grow: What the Bible Reveals about Personal Growth.* Grand Rapids, MI: Zondervan, 2001. Print.

Martin, Ralph P. *Worship in the Early Church.* Grand Rapids: Eerdmans, 1974. Print.

Smith, F. LaGard. *The Cultural Church.* Nashville, TN: 20th Century Christian, 1992. Print.

Smith, F. LaGard. *Radical Restoration: A Call for Pure and Simple Christianity.* Nashville, TN: Cotswold Pub., 2001. Print.

Viola, Frank, and George Barna. *Pagan Christianity?: Exploring the Roots of Our Church Practices.* Carol Stream, IL: Barna, 2008. Print.

Viola, Frank. *Reimagining Church: Pursuing the Dream of Organic Christianity.* Colorado Springs, CO: David C. Cook, 2008. Print.

White, James F. *A Brief History of Christian Worship.* Nashville: Abingdon, 1993. Print.

ABOUT THE AUTHOR

Originally from Phoenix Arizona, Tom Mann lives in Temple Terrace, Florida with his wife of over 30 years, Meladie Walker Mann. Tom has two children. He has a Bachelor's degree in Education, a Master's degree in English and a Doctorate in Law. He is a teacher, a lawyer and a mediator. He has taught English and Law to youth and adults at all levels, from junior high school to postgraduate levels. Tom Mann has also written a book on the Psalms entitled *Exploring Psalms*.

www.ingramcontent.com/pod-product-compliance
Lightning Source LLC
Chambersburg PA
CBHW080935040426
42443CB00015B/3417